The Wendish Crusade, 1147

The Wendish Crusade of 1147, one of the Northern Crusades and a part of the Second Crusade, took place at a critical phase in the evolution of crusading rhetoric. The initiators and apologists of the campaign employed rhetorical devices to justify the occupation of a region and conversion of a population under the auspices of a crusade. A detailed examination of the primary sources shows that the justification of a crusade against apostates was not only a German endeavour, or the pope's will, but a political reality of the twelfth century. Therefore, the attitude of the papacy is shown to be reactive rather than proactive.

Mihai Dragnea completed his doctoral research at the Romanian Academy ('Nicolae Iorga' Institute of History). The thesis entitled *Mission and Crusade in the Wendish Territory, 12th Century* was published in Romanian in 2019. His research interests include the relations between Germans and Wends during the High Middle Ages, with a focus on crusading and conversion. He is the current President of the Balkan History Association.

The Wendish Crusade, 1147
The Development of Crusading Ideology in the Twelfth Century

Mihai Dragnea

LONDON AND NEW YORK

First published 2020 by Routledge

2 Park Square, Milton Park, Abingdon, Oxon OX14 4RN
605 Third Avenue, New York, NY 10017

Routledge is an imprint of the Taylor & Francis Group, an informa business

First issued in paperback 2021

Copyright © 2020 Mihai Dragnea

The right of Mihai Dragnea to be identified as author of this work has been asserted by him in accordance with sections 77 and 78 of the Copyright, Designs and Patents Act 1988.

All rights reserved. No part of this book may be reprinted or reproduced or utilised in any form or by any electronic, mechanical, or other means, now known or hereafter invented, including photocopying and recording, or in any information storage or retrieval system, without permission in writing from the publishers.

Notice:
Product or corporate names may be trademarks or registered trademarks, and are used only for identification and explanation without intent to infringe.

Publisher's Note

The publisher has gone to great lengths to ensure the quality of this reprint but points out that some imperfections in the original copies may be apparent.

British Library Cataloguing-in-Publication Data
A catalogue record for this book is available from the British Library

Library of Congress Cataloging-in-Publication Data
CIP data for this book has been requested.

ISBN: 978-0-367-36696-4 (hbk)
ISBN: 978-1-03-217746-5 (pbk)
DOI: 10.4324/9780429350849

Typeset in Times New Roman
by Newgen Publishing UK

Contents

	Foreword	vi
	List of abbreviations	viii
1	Introduction	1
2	Crusade ideology in northern Europe and Bernard of Clairvaux	5
3	Forced conversion and the new canon law (*ius novum*)	19
4	The conquest of a pagan territory blessed by the church	30
5	Expanding the crusading ideal on the eastern shore of the Baltic	39
	Conclusion	64
	Index of names	66

Foreword

The medieval crusades in the Baltic during the twelfth century have received increasing scholarly interest during recent years, and research has changed significantly. New questions, new perspectives, new contexts and new academic traditions have been applied in the interpretation of sources of which the great majority have been known for a very long time.

Much research in the twentieth century had strong nationalistic agendas, expressed openly or as an undertone that coloured the analyses and favoured some historical agents at the expense of others. German and Polish historians had often strikingly different understandings of the crusades and their justification, and Soviet historiography in the USSR and in the Baltic states could describe the crusades in the Baltic as Western aggression solely for political and economic reasons.

The great political changes around 1990 and the independence of the Baltic states led to a renewed interest in the medieval history and in these areas' incorporation into a common European culture, but also to attempts to understand violence and warfare as caused not only by material but also by ideological concerns. War for values and not only to secure political independence was discussed in military academies and among political decision makers, with repercussions and reflections also in historical research.

Were crusaders from Germany and Scandinavia fighting only to gain more land and tribute, or were they motivated by a desire to convert infidels to Christianity? Was there a contradiction between converting with peaceful preaching and with sharp swords, or were the two methods applied simultaneously? Were crusaders driven by other strong emotions, such as an urge to take revenge on infidels, and to what extent did crusaders care about the regulations and prescriptions of the Church and ecclesiastical theoreticians?

These are some of the important questions raised in this book by Dr Mihai Dragnea, who treats the Baltic crusades in a broader context. The specific course of events was not only dependent upon political circumstances in the lands around the Baltic Sea, but also on the crusading movement in general. And important theological discussions about the use of force in conversion were raised first in the Baltic, but the results were applied very fast in other crusading areas far away from the north.

Dr Kurt Villads Jensen
Centre for Medieval Studies, Stockholm University

List of abbreviations

BRG *Bibliotheca Rerum Germanicarum*
CIC *Corpus Iuris Canonici*
MGH *Monumenta Germaniae Historica*

Subdivided by series:
SS *Scriptores*
SRG *Scriptores Rerum Germanicarum*
PL *Patrologia Latina*

1 Introduction

Our main question is how to justify a crusade that did not aim at recovering the Holy Land, but to conquer a region where the Christian presence was temporary.* This study addresses the discussions about the relation between warfare and ideology. The initiators of the Saxon expedition against the Wends and later apologists employed moral and legal arguments to justify the conquest of a region under the auspices of a crusade. Therefore in this study we will focus on the evolution of crusading ideology and practice according to political contexts in twelfth-century Germany.

The chief instigator of the Second Crusade was the Cistercian abbot Bernard of Clairvaux, who tried to define the Saxon campaign across the Elbe as part of a great battle against all the enemies of Christendom. The crusade was called by Pope Eugene III as a response to the fall of the County of Edessa in 1144. Therefore Bernard recruited first the French King Louis VII and then the German King Conrad III to raise an army and reconquer Edessa from the Muslims. The Saxon nobles refused to participate and received papal authorization to organize a military campaign against the Wends.

In determining why the Saxons refused to march to the Holy Land, it is first necessary to place these events in a broader political context. We must therefore look at the men who led the campaign and their greedy desire to grab Wendish land instead of crusading in the Holy Land. In other words, the Saxon nobles were interested more in conquering land than winning souls. Accordingly, we must understand that for the Saxon nobility, the acquisition of land played an essential role in motivating knights to go on crusade and not to follow the opportunity for spiritual rewards in the Holy Land. Thus for the Saxons, a unity of purpose created by material and spiritual rewards does not match the reality of the situation.

The military campaign against the Wends is usually referred to as the Wendish Crusade. However, modern scholarship has questioned not only the existence of some common plans for the papacy to take on all of its enemies but also the crusading idea in the twelfth century. This is why the terminology most often used to understand the Wendish Crusade is disputed. In this book I intend to show that the Wendish Crusade is a significant turning point in crusading historiography. The difficulty that Bernard and other clerics faced in defining its purpose is highlighted in primary sources. There is no doubt that for Bernard and Eugene III, the Wendish expedition was seen in the broad framework of the Second Crusade. Bernard and later commentators reinterpreted Saxon traditions to conform to the general idea of crusading.

The Wendish Crusade took place in a critical phase in the evolution of crusade rhetoric. What the existing scholarship has not proved is the importance of the Wendish Crusade in the legitimacy of conquest and conversion of a population. Both moral and legal justifications were expressed in canon law. Our perspective argues that the Wendish Crusade offers some interesting clues to new developments in crusading ideology, as well as forced conversion. The initiators and apologists of the campaign employed rhetorical devices to justify the occupation of a region and conversion of a population under the auspices of a crusade. A comparison of the primary sources will be made to show that the justification of a crusade against apostates was not only a German endeavour, or the pope's will, but a political reality of the twelfth century. Thus the attitude of the papacy was reactive rather than proactive.

An essential aspect is the relationship of the Saxons with their eastern neighbours. The first major records for the relationship between the two groups come from the reign of Charlemagne. In the Frankish campaign against the pagan Saxons, the Wends play an important role as allies of the Franks. As a reward, they receive from Charlemagne a large part of the Holstein region, which was inhabited by Saxons at that time. This is why the Saxon margraves and dukes sought revenge against the Wends, who were often used by the Franks to secure their borderlands. Starting with the first king of the Saxon line, Henry I, the Saxon nobles attempted to expand their realm all the way to the Oder by creating an eastern march and bringing under their control the whole territory up to the Polish border.

Missionary activity in northern Europe was highlighted by authors like Adam of Bremen (eleventh century) or Helmold of Bosau (twelfth century). Their narratives belong to a genre known as *gesta episcoporum* ("the deeds of bishops"), which is distinct from texts describing the deeds of kings or the history of *gentes*.¹ The conversion was temporary and was largely due to the military campaigns undertaken by the Saxon margraves. These campaigns were aided by the conversion of some of the Wendish leaders (e.g. the Obotrite dynasty of Nako), who maintained a tolerant political climate towards the Saxon ecclesiastical organization. The right of the Saxon margraves to conquer and administer the region across the Elbe was possible through tributary relations with Wendish leaders.²

In the late tenth century, the Wends, dissatisfied with the heavy tribute they had to pay to the Saxon nobility, rebelled. Their opposition to Saxon domination led to a mass apostasy and abandonment of the ecclesiastical centres on the eastern side of the Elbe. These insurrections put an end to the process of conversion for some time. During the first half of the eleventh century, the Ottonians and the Salians tried to regain control beyond the Elbe. Otto III's campaigns were an attempt to protect the fragile remains of Christianity. To be part again of the *imperium Christianum*, it was not sufficient to submit to the Saxon dukes and pay tribute. It was also necessary to submit to the Saxon Church, into which they had been integrated in the time of Otto the Great and to which they still belonged. Suffragan dioceses of the church of Magdeburg, notably the bishoprics of Brandenburg and Havelberg, were abandoned until the twelfth century. Similar insurrections against the Saxon ecclesiastical authorities across the Elbe occured during the eleventh century.³ In some cases, Wendish princes such as Gottschalk supported the conversion process. After his death, missionary activity resumed only in the first half of the twelfth century; it was supported by illustrious bishops such as Otto of Bamberg and Vicelin of Oldenburg.⁴

Notes

* The research was conducted at the Institute of History and Archaeology (University of Tartu) and was funded by the Romanian Cultural Institute; 'Lucian Blaga' Postdoctoral Fellowship, no. 7177/29.05.2018.
1 For recent overviews regarding the missionary activity described by these chroniclers, see Jezierski 2018: 259–263, Jezierski 2017: 115–124, Garipzanov 2011: 13–29, Kaljundi 2008: 113–127, Scior 2002.
2 Althoff 1999: 278–288.
3 For the Wendish apostasy and the Saxon reaction, see Dragnea 2016: 57–58, Janson 2010: 11–30, Kahl 1955: 161–193, 360–401.
4 For the conversion of Pomerania by Otto of Bamberg, see Dragnea 2015: 37–48, Guth 1992: 13–23, Bartlett 1985: 185–201. For the missionary activities of Vicelin of Oldenburg, see Hoffmann 1976: 115–142.

References

Althoff, Gerd. 1999. 'Saxony and the Elbe Slavs in the Tenth Century'. In *The New Cambridge Medieval History, vol. III c.900–c.1024*, ed. Timothy Reuter, 267–292. Cambridge: Cambridge University Press.

Bartlett, Robert. 1985. 'The Conversion of a Pagan Society in the Middle Ages'. *History* 70 (229): 185–201.

Dragnea, Mihai. 2016. 'Divine Vengeance and Human Justice in the Wendish Crusade of 1147'. *Collegium Medievale* 29: 49–82.

Dragnea, Mihai. 2015. 'Otto din Bamberg: Reformă Monastică şi Misiune Apostolică'. In *Timp, societate şi identitate culturală. „Miniaturi" istorice*, eds. Ileana Căzan and Bogdan Mateescu, 25–48. Cluj-Napoca: Academia Română – Centrul de Studii Transilvane.

Garipzanov, Ildar H. 2011. 'Christianity and Paganism in Adam of Bremen's Narrative'. In *Historical Narratives and Christian Identity on a European Periphery: Early History Writing in Northern, East-Central, and Eastern Europe (c.1070–1200)*, ed. Ildar H. Garipzanov, 13–29. Turnhout: Brepols.

Guth, Klaus. 1992. 'The Pomeranian Missionary Journeys of Otto I of Bamberg and the Crusade Movement of the Eleventh to Twelfth Centuries'. In *The Second Crusade and the Cistercians*, ed. Michael Gervers, 13–23. New York: Palgrave Macmillan.

Hoffmann, Eric. 1976. 'Vicelin und die Neubegründung des Bistums Oldenburg/ Lübeck'. In *Lübeck 1226: Reichsfreiheit und frühe Stadt*, eds. O. Ahlers et al., 115–142. Lübeck: Hansisches Verlagskontor Scheffler.

Janson, Henrik. 2010. 'What Made the Pagans Pagans?' In *Medieval Christianitas: Different Regions, 'Faces', Approaches*, eds. T. Stepanov and G. Kazakov, 11–30. Sofia: Voenno izdatelstvo.

Jezierski, Wojtek. 2018. 'Feelings during Sieges: Fear, Trust, and Emotional Bonding on the Missionary and Crusader Baltic Rim, 12th–13th Centuries'. *Frühmittelalterliche Studien* 52: 253–281.

Jezierski, Wojtek. 2017. 'Fears, Sights and Slaughter: Expressions of Fright and Disgust in the Baltic Missionary Historiography (11th–13th centuries)'. In *Tears, Sighs and Laughter: Expressions of Emotions in the Middle Ages*, eds. P. Förnegård et al., 109–137. Stockholm: Vitterhets.

Kahl, Hans-Dietrich. 1955. 'Compellere intrare. Die Wendenpolitik Bruns von Querfurt im Lichte hochmittelalterlichen Missions- und Völkerrechts'. *Zeitschrift für Ostforschung* 4: 161–193, 360–401.

Kaljundi, Linda. 2008. 'Waiting for the Barbarians: Reconstruction of Otherness in the Saxon Missionary and Crusading Chronicles, 11th–13th Centuries'. In *The Medieval Chronicle*, 5, ed. Erik Kooper, 113–127. Amsterdam: Rodopi.

Scior, Volker. 2002. *Das Eigene und das Fremde: Identität und Fremdheit in den Chroniken Adams von Bremen, Helmolds von Bosau und Arnolds von Lübeck*. Berlin: De Gruyter.

2 Crusade ideology in northern Europe and Bernard of Clairvaux

The First Crusade, proclaimed by Pope Urban II for the liberation of the Holy Land in 1095, was defined as a spiritual and military action in which "taking the cross" meant engaging in a war against the "enemies of Christ".[1] Jerusalem, liberated in 1099, was indispensable in the discourse of contemporary clergy. Its spiritual significance was also felt among the clergy of the archdioceses of Hamburg-Bremen and Magdeburg, responsible for the conversion of the Wends. The enthusiasm that dominated the hearts of the participants in the First Crusade (1096–1099) was remarkably widespread in Latin Christendom. The papacy and apologists spread the idea that the struggle against infidels was the guarantee of obtaining forgiveness of sins and the recognition of divine mercy.[2]

The most important preacher of the Second Crusade was Bernard, abbot of Clairvaux. At that time, Bernard was one of the most influential theologians of the Western Church. His sermons had reached all corners of Latin Christendom. Helmold of Bosau, the main chronicler of the Wendish Crusade, called him "the most notorious" (*famosissimo illo*).[3] Through his oratorical skill, the Cistercian abbot succeeded in conveying the papal message to European kings. Bernard's speech in Frankfurt (13 March 1147) and the encyclical issued by Pope Eugene III on 11 April (*Divini dispensatione*) opened a new front of the crusade.[4] The Saxons were urged to join the crusade movement by fighting against the Wends, instead of going to the Holy Land. By doing this, the Saxons received the same spiritual privileges as crusaders in the east.[5] The emergence of the crusade phenomenon in the Baltic region has been easily identified with the two major interests of the Saxon clergy and nobility: the desire to convert and subdue the Wends, both fuelled by the ideology of Holy War.

The Cistercian abbot had not instructed the crusaders in the East to kill the Muslims if they should refuse to convert, yet in 1147 he seemed to be proposing such measures across the Elbe. Somehow, Muslims and Jews shared with Christians certain basic values which protected them against arbitrary violence. In overriding the restrictions he had previously placed on the use of force, Bernard also departed radically from his peaceful arguments regarding the conversion of Jews. However, his vision on Muslims and Jews was not a reflection of papal policy or canon law, but a means to advance his personal spiritual desire of union with God.[6]

Bernard's so-called peaceful position towards Muslims and Jews can be found in the reform of Benedictine monasticism that caused the foundation of the Cistercian Order. The articulation of crusading ideology was connected with the foundation of the Cistercian Order as well as the Templars. The Cistercians were not a military order like the Templars, but Bernard was active in the propagation of crusading ideology among its members. The Templars had a special position within the history of the development of the concept of knighthood. This is why the Order of the Temple was depicted as the only institution able to regenerate knighthood. Among the religious authorities who agreed with this idea was Bernard.[7] In a treatise (*De laude novae militae*, "In Praise of the New Knighthood") written between 1129 and 1135 and addressed to Hugh of Payens, Bernard expressed his support for the Order. In the treatise, Bernard defined two categories of knighthood: one was inspired by the monastic ideals of Cistercian reform, and the other by the secular concepts of knighthood. Thus Bernard depicted secular knighthood as an evil, in opposition to the Templars, who were called the "new knights" (*novum militiae genus*). For Bernard, the Templars are the true knights and their power is both physical and spiritual and therefore they are able to fight with the enemies of Christ. Therefore, if a Templar fought "for a good reason, the issue of his fight can never be evil; and likewise the results can never be considered good if the reason was evil and the intentions perverse".[8]

De laude novae militiae reflects the evolution from a traditional so-called peaceful mission of individuals to an organized and violent mission supported by the sword. It also reflects the ideal of Christian chivalry in Bernard's eyes and the specific code of behaviour for the Templars. As Bernard suggested, a war is only just if it is fought for a reason that is justified in terms of theology and law. So not the nature of the warfare itself, but the intentions of those who launched it were analyzed. If the intentions came from the warrior's heart, and not from his material interests, a war could be accepted by the Church.[9] This meant that a forced conversion could be moral only if crusaders were inflamed by the zeal of God. The Templars and many theologians shared this outlook. Christian zeal would force the infidels to convert and thus divine vengeance could be avoided.

This specific attitude of the Templars also influenced the knights who participated in the Wendish Crusade of 1147. Helmold does not mention whether the crusader armies led by Henry the Lion and Albert the Bear, count of Ballenstedt and margrave of the North March (from 1157 Brandenburg),[10] included knights. Yet the Obotrite Prince Niklot, against whom the crusade was directed, was killed by the knights of Henry the Lion in 1160. Then he divided the Obotrite realm and put his knights in possession of it.[11] Helmold's omission of the knights' participation in the Crusade against the Wends was not an accident. For the chronicler, the crusade was a failure because it did not provide a lasting conversion. He expressed disappointment with the Saxon duke, whose material interests had stopped the process of conversion. The same vision can be found in a letter written in 1149 by Wibald, the abbot of Stavelot and Corvey to Bishop Bernard I of Hildesheim[12] and in the Anchin continuation of the chronicle of Sigebert of Gembloux (d. 1112).[13]

The subsequent military campaigns organized by Henry the Lion had the purpose of conquering Niklot's territory, while conversion played a secondary role. Helmold of Bosau acted as an agent of the *libertas ecclesiae*. There is no doubt that he supported the Archdiocese of Hamburg-Bremen in the conflict with the Saxon duke. Most mentions of the missionary activity concern the clerics from the suffragan dioceses. The only Saxon noble who supported the missionary activity was Count Adolf II of Holstein. Probably Helmold understood that the crusade ideology preached by Bernard would not bring positive results for the conversion process across the Elbe. After all, he knew very well about the previous attempts to convert the Wends. Since he lived within a missionary community, he had an understanding of the conversion process both in theory and practice.

However, the sacralization of knighthood made possible the emergence of the idea of holy war. As long as served the interests of the papacy, often identified with the interests of secular leaders, the actions of the Templars were sanctified. Secular knights could have a similar status as long as they "took the cross" against the enemies of the Church. Only the papacy, and not the secular leaders, was able to identify the Church's enemies and proclaim a crusade against them. In fact, the pope wanted to limit the royal power only to the temporal sphere. Since his spiritual power came straight from God, he believed that he was the only legitimate authority to establish a social order.[14]

Bernard of Clairvaux supported the idea that crusades could be directed against all enemies of Christ, including those in the Iberian Peninsula and north-eastern Germany. The ideological background of the Wendish Crusade was set out by Bernard in his letter from Frankfurt in March 1147. The letter has led to many debates among historians about the theology of the Crusades. By using a similar rhetoric to that in his treatise for the Templars, Bernard forbade the receiving of tribute and any peace agreement until the Wends were subdued.[15] The Cistercian abbot was aware of the Saxons' intentions. Their interest in money rather than conversion is confirmed by Helmold of Bosau,[16] Vincent of Prague[17] and the author of *Annales Palidenses*, written between 1182 and 1197 at the Premonstratensian monastery of Pöhlde. In the latter source there are reports on the discussions between the Saxon nobles, who had already begun to share out the Wendish land which had not yet been conquered.[18]

However, the receiving of tribute meant that the Saxon duke would recognize the Obotrite pagan state. In this situation, the conversion of the Wends would be a consequence of his political actions, and not the wish of God (*Deo auctore* war). For Bernard, the conversion had to be accomplished by the Church of Hamburg-Bremen. All bishoprics in north-eastern Germany abandoned after the Wendish insurrections were suffragans of Hamburg-Bremen. Thus the task of conversion could be undertaken only by the clergy of Hamburg-Bremen. By tradition, since the Carolingian period, the archdiocese of Hamburg-Bremen was responsible for the conversion of the northern peoples.

Another reason for Bernard's involvement in the conversion was the conflict between the archdiocese of Hamburg-Bremen and the Saxon duke, Henry the Lion. For decades, archbishops such as Adalbero and Hartwig I had been supported by the papacy in their conflict with the Saxon duke. On the eve of the 1147 crusade, Henry the Lion was having difficulty in regaining all the territories that belonged to the Billungs. In 1144, Count Rudolf II of Stade was killed. His territories between Weser and Oder became the property of his brother Hartwig, then the Provost of Bremen Cathedral. To secure his new property against Henry the Lion, Hartwig attempted to place it under the archdiocese of Hamburg-Bremen, ruled by him from 1148. When Adalbero tried to defend the legitimacy of the offer to Hartwig, Henry the Lion intervened and confiscated the territories. Another cause of conflict between Henry the Lion and the archdiocese of Hamburg-Bremen was the right to appoint bishops in the suffragan dioceses. That is why, at Frankfurt, the Saxon duke expressed his interest in the Obotrite realm and the Duchy of Bavaria.

Bernard's position regarding the purpose of the Wendish Crusade of 1147 has been much debated. According to him, the Saxons ought to convert or exterminate the Wends.[19] Similar connotations were used elsewhere in the letter. This proposal of "baptism or death" suggests a radical position regarding the canonical regulation of conversion. It was emphasized that Bernard discussed killing the Wends or at least destroying their pagan customs and political entity. There is no doubt that Bernard gave his permission for forced conversion.[20]

In Bernard's speech we can identify two major targets: Wendish society (idols, shrines, sacrifices, polygamy) and the Obotrite political entity. For him, the Obotrite *natio* included these two main components. Therefore it is very likely that forced conversion included physical and psychological torture, starvation, blackmail and any other kind of aggression. In this context, the baptism would be valid if the convert had given his consent. It is hard to believe that in these critical circumstances, a person would not accept baptism and follow the sacraments. In that way, "with the help of God" the Obotrite *natio* would be destroyed, and not its people.[21] This would clear the way for missionaries. The immoral pagan customs would be replaced with the Christian virtues. Through the sacraments, the Wends would receive the grace of the Holy Spirit and thus would be connected to Christianity. Bernard, aware of their previous religious and political apostasy, sought to create a new political and social context in order to sustain their conversion. This could be possible if the crusaders fought against those Wends who had remained pagans in order to protect the newly converted.

Bernard's main goal was to annihilate the Wendish way of life. The Wends had to be isolated from what defined them as a social and political entity outside Christianity. The *ritus* that Bernard was talking about was the heart of Wendish society. The political independence of Obotrite leaders was not possible without maintaining their own rite. By accepting the Christian rite, the Obotrite elites would have become dependent on ecclesiastical authorities and the ability to govern their subjects would have declined considerably. Bernard understood that the destruction of the rite meant the annihilation of the Obotrite *natio*. Idol worship, sacrifices, polygamy and any other non-Christian customs were forbidden. In this case, the Obotrite elites would have no alternative but to accept baptism. Keeping the Wends within Christianity required a favourable political context for both Saxons and ecclesiastical authorities. The history of the relations between the Saxons and their eastern neighbours shows us that every time the latter had the opportunity to become more independent, they seized it without reservation.

As Friedrich Lotter convincingly argued, the Wends could live within their own state (*natio*) only if their leaders were willing to convert. An independent *natio* and *ritus* would not have been accepted. However, if the leaders refused, their own statehood would be destroyed (*natio deleatur*) and they would be subjected to Christian rulers.[22] Therefore we believe that Eugene III and Bernard supported the political autonomy of the Obotrite leaders if they were willing to convert and accept the Saxon duke as their lord. Bernard was aware of the alliance between Count Adolf II of Holstein, a faithful vassal of Henry the Lion, and the Obotrite Prince Niklot.[23] This friendship allowed Niklot to be more independent. Yet the territory of one of his eastern tributaries – the Circipanians – was claimed not only by the Saxon duke, but also by Albert the Bear. During the siege of Demmin, which was the most important Circipanian stronghold, some vassals of Henry the Lion and Albert the Bear, who led the army, said to each other: "Is not the land we are devastating our land, and the people we are fighting our people? Why are we, then, found to be our own enemies and the destroyers of our own incomes? Does not this loss fall back on our lords?"[24]

We know that in 1143, just one year after Henry the Lion received the Duchy of Saxony from King Conrad III, another Obotrite prince, Pribislav of Wagria, became a tributary of Adolf. His realm was reduced to a small territory in north-eastern Wagria.[25] Around 1156, Pribislav paid tribute not only to Adolf, but also to Henry the Lion. When Bishop Gerold of Oldenburg rebuked Pribislav for the bad treatment inflicted on Danish prisoners, the Obotrite prince complained that the tribute paid to the Saxon duke (a thousand marks) was much higher than that offered to Adolf. In reply, the bishop said that the exploitation of the Wends is not a sin, because they worship idols and therefore they are regarded as having no legitimate rights like the Saxons. To avoid this status, the Wends were advised to become subject to Christianity.[26] It is very likely that Pribislav and his subjects had to exploit the Danish captives in order to compensate for the losses caused by the heavy tribute. In fact the captives were slaves, sold to the Wendish nobility, who forced them to perform hard work. The words of Gerold show that for the Saxon ecclesiastical authorities, the Wends were outcasts. They were called idolaters because they rejected the Saxons' Christ. To be considered and treated as a Christian, not only faith and sacraments, but also the payment of tithes was required. Their inclusion within Christian Saxon society freed them afterwards from the burden of the tribute. Pribislav had an interest in converting and staying Christian. In this way, he could maintain his title and posessions. For the Saxon clerics, this conversion would not have violated canon law.

Crusade ideology and Bernard of Clairvaux 11

Helmold does not tell us too much about the political relationship between Adolf and Niklot. All we know is that after having occupied much of Wagria, Adolf sent messengers with gifts to Niklot to conclude a peace treaty.[27] According to the historical record, most of the Wendish leaders had been tributaries of the Saxon dukes and margraves since the Ottonians. Yet we do not know if Niklot became a tributary of Adolf or his vassal, Henry the Lion, until 1147. The relationship between Adolf and Niklot was based on friendship, fidelity and some verbal "pledges" (*sponsionis*) made by Niklot. In this case, besides the possibility of paying tribute like many of his predecessors, Niklot might have been obliged to provide military support to Adolf and prevent other Wendish raids, but not to accept baptism and to convert his people. There were no other means than military ones that would have coerced him into accepting baptism. As long as he offered his material and military support, the Obotrite prince would have had cultural and social independence.

The political relationship between Niklot and the Saxon duke is more clearly revealed only after 1147. In 1151, two of Niklot's eastern tributaries – the Kicini and the Circipanians – revolted, refusing to pay the tribute. To solve this issue, Niklot needed the approval of Henry's wife, Duchess Clementia, who ruled in Lüneburg while the duke was away. Clementia ordered Adolf and his vassals, the Holsatians and Sturmarians, to give support to Niklot to suppress the rebellion.[28] In 1157, Henry the Lion ordered Niklot to help the Danish King Sweyn III to return to Denmark.[29] The hierarchy of power across the Elbe was conditioned by the needs of the Saxon duke and Niklot's military power. Helmold tells us that in 1159, Emperor Frederick I (1155–1190) has asked his cousin, Henry the Lion, to conclude a new peace treaty with Niklot and his subjects. The peace cost Frederick over a thousand marks of silver. In addition, the Obotrite prince had to bring all his ships in Lübeck to be delivered to the duke's delegate. Within the treaty concluded with Henry the Lion, Niklot had to make peace with the Danish King Valdemar I. We do not know how this treaty would have been implemented. The only thing we know is that the treaty was ratified by an oath (*iuramento*).[30] A much more severe treaty was concluded in 1168, when the same Valdemar I invaded Rugia and conquered its religious and political stronghold, Arkona. Saxo Grammaticus tells us that the following conditions were needed to conclude the treaty: the release of all Christian captives, confiscation of the temple treasure, military support, tribute (forty silver pieces annually for each yoke of oxen) and offering all the farms and estates of the gods to the Danish clergy. Besides these severe material conditions, Valdemar forced the

Rugians to follow Christianity "according to the Danish rite".[31] The tribute seems to be a consequence of a form of illegitimate Christianity that the Rugians followed. They were not real pagans; they had another religion (*aliena religio*) which was regarded as an apostasy based on a mixture of Christian and pagan superstitions. The Rugians relapsed from the faith and followed false idols. They refused contact with God through the Danish ecclesiastical authorities. For the clergy, it was a rejection of the Danish God, which they had accepted about three decades before.[32] This status made them considered to be religious and political apostates. Therefore it was fully justifiable to force the Rugians to return to the Danish Church they had once accepted. This meant that a forced conversion would not violate the terms of *jus canonicum*. This was a just vision since God Himself had taken revenge on the Rugians. Those who embraced Christianity were supported by miracles, while those who insulted the Christian faith were crippled.[33] In this context we should not be surprised that Archbishop Eskil of Lund justified the conquest of Rugia by saying that the submission to the Danish Church was a victory more important than receiving tribute. This measure was seen as an act of piety (*pietas*) which would have prevented the killing of the new subjects.[34]

There is no doubt that at Frankfurt, while preaching the crusade, Bernard saw Adolf as a threat to conversion. The count may have not believed that forced conversion was the right solution. He did not see the campaign against the Wends as a crusade, as it was presented by Bernard. Therefore his involvement in a crusade against his ally needed endorsement by a man of Bernard's sanctity.[35] There is no information about his participation among the crusaders in the first army. However, his objection could not have cancelled Bernard's plans. Only his lord the duke was able to make that decision. What we know from Helmold is that when Niklot heard that an army was ready to march against him, he sent messengers to Adolf to ask his help. The count refused, saying that his support might give offence to Henry the Lion and the rest of the Saxon nobles who agreed to join the crusade. In response, Niklot accused Adolf of destroying an old friendship and violating the treaty they had previously concluded and that had brought peace and prosperity to Wagria.[36]

Bernard hoped for a full integration of the Wends within the *imperium Christianum*. For him, *natio* meant the political authority of the Obotrite elites. His position followed the history of relationships between Saxons and Wends. Thus, the pope would not challenge the legal position; the autonomy of the Obotrite leaders was recognized by the Saxon nobles as long as they paid tribute. The owners of the Wendish lands would be the Saxon nobles, and the Obotrite leaders would be their tributaries. If they did not accept conversion, the leaders would have lost their titles and possessions and the Wends would be subjected directly to the Saxon nobles. However, in 1147, after much of the Obotrite territory was occupied by the Saxons, the tributary relationship with Prince Niklot was restored. In addition to paying the tribute, Niklot agreed that he would convert to Christianity.[37] He may have imposed this on his subjects, or at least the Obotrite elites. Helmold stated that in 1148, after the marriage with Clementia of Zähringen, Henry ruled "over the whole country of the Slavs".[38] Three years later, before Henry went to Bavaria to reclaim the duchy, he gave Count Adolf "custody" of the Wendish territory.[39]

The Saxon duke's right to wage war against the Obotrite princes is confirmed by Helmold. It is very likely that the tributary relation between Henry the Lion and Niklot was certified by a written agreement or an oath. If Niklot did not respect one of his obligations, then the Saxon duke would have had the right to intervene militarily. After Niklot's death, almost all his possessions were divided among the Saxon nobles. The territories that remained under the rule of Niklot's legitimate son Pribislav were those in the east, inhabited by Kessinians (*terra Kycinorum*) and Circipanians (*terra Circipanorum*), which initially belonged to the Lutici. The only remaining fortress under Pribislav's dominion was Werle, located on the Warnow River. Dissatisfied with this situation, Pribislav and his brother Vratislav tried to reconquer the Obotrite territory, which Henry the Lion acquired through the "right of war".[40]

The political climate in the Obotrite area had changed considerably after 1147. For a short time, Niklot was faithful to Henry the Lion. It is very likely that the conversion began in this "peaceful" context (*pax erat in Slavia*). Without the duke's approval, in 1149, Archbishop Hartwig of Hamburg-Bremen restored the suffragan dioceses of Oldenburg and Mecklenburg. Two missionary bishops were ordained, Vicelin in Oldenburg and Emmehard in Mecklenburg.[41] The two bishops were ready to accept forced conversion, even if it violated canon law and Bernard's previous vision concerning the Crusades. It is possible that the Cistercian abbot had in mind the physical destruction of the Wendish pagan culture, not the killing of people. In describing the mission of the Saxon crusaders, Bernard avoided flouting the doctrinal stipulation that conversion could not be forced. In other words, Bernard extended the crusader's authority from the defence of the Holy Land to the destruction of an enemy territory, in order to encourage the Wends to convert.

The idea of crusade conceived in Frankfurt by Bernard was modified by Eugene III in a characteristic way. The pope would have shared

Bernard's expectation regarding the crusade, but his vision on conversion is ambiguous. The choice of "baptism or death" emphasized by Bernard demanded full integration into Christendom. In the encyclical issued on April 1147, Eugene stated that the conversion of the Wends and other "pagans of the North" was to be achieved by the crusade. With the Lord's help, the Wends would be subjected to the Christian religion (*eos Christiane religioni subjugare*).[42] The vision of Eugene and that of Bernard were interconnected. For the author of the *Magdeburg Annals*, composed at the monastery of Berge in Magdeburg in the last quarter of the twelfth century, it was obvious that a full integration into Christendom would have been possible only through the physical subjection of the Wends. However, the author did not mention whether the Wendish leaders would have been subjected, or the entire population. What we know from him is that the purpose of the expedition against the Wends was "to subject them to Christianity, or, with God's help, fully exterminate them".[43]

Eugene did not discuss the subject of conversion. More than that, he did not define the purpose of the expedition against the Wends. In fact, Eugene did not show much interest in conversion. This lack of interest should be explained in the context of papal policy. With few exceptions, the popes of the early and central Middle Ages did not initiate or plan missionary projects.[44] What is clear in Eugene's encyclical is the direct association of the campaign against the Wends with those planned for the Levant and the Iberian Peninsula. Besides that, the Saxon crusaders benefited from the same privileges as those granted to the crusaders in the East. In order to maintain the sacred character of the campaign highlighted by Bernard, Eugene appointed Bishop Anselm of Havelberg as papal legate.[45] Some clerics like Helmold and the author of the *Annales Palidenses* did not refer to a significant number of knights ready to achieve remission of sins or any kind of spiritual salvation. This would be explained by the fact that Helmold and the author of the *Annales Palidenses* believed that the Saxon nobles understood the campaign against the Wends as an act of conquest. Their criticism was argued by the fact that Henry the Lion waged a war based on material interests and did not care too much about conversion. If, after the campaign, the Wends would be fully integrated into Christendom, perhaps the two clerics would have praised the initiative of forced conversion. The writing of the *Annales Palidenses* began in 1182, when Henry the Lion was exiled by his cousin, the Emperor Frederick I. The author's attitude should be placed within the context of conflict between Staufen and Welfs. It is very likely that the author supported the emperor in the conflict with the Saxon duke. On the other hand Wibald, the abbot of

Stavelot and Corvey who was one of the spiritual leaders of the second crusader army led by Albert the Bear, emphasized the remission of sins granted for those who fought against the Wends.[46] It seems that this army achieved more spiritual results. In *Chronica principum Saxoniae et monumenta Brandenburgensia* it was stated that the spiritual leaders of the second army who took the cross against the pagan Wends managed to convert many of them to the Christian faith by baptism.[47]

However, the encyclical issued by Eugene is the first official document in which a pope approved the use of force against the pagans in order to convert them. From the pope's discourse we notice that he directed a military campaign designed to achieve a forced conversion, rather than creating a context for a missionary activity. More than that, Eugene recognized the legitimacy of Saxon rule over the Wendish territories. According to tradition, the Saxon ecclesiastical authorities within the archdiocese of Hamburg-Bremen were responsible for the conversion of the Wends and Scandinavians. The missionaries who preached across the Elbe were often supported by the Saxon nobles. This is why a subjection to Christianity was first a subjection to Saxon nobles, the protagonists of the Crusade. The pope did not express the alternative of extermination if the Wends refused to convert. Nor did he forbid the conclusion of peace treaties with the Wendish leaders.

Notes

1 Cecilia Gaposchkin makes a distinction between the ceremony for departing crusaders and the ritual moment when a crusader "took up the cross". This act was made before the military act and involves a *votum crucis*. Gaposchkin 2013: 44–47.
2 For more details regarding the records of the Council of Clermont, see Niall and Gerish 2003: 139–148.
3 Helmold of Bosau 1937: I, 79.
4 The literature on Baltic crusades and missionary warfare has grown markedly in the last two decades. An important overview regarding the ideological background of the crusade phenomenon is Bysted et al. 2012.
5 Bernard of Clairvaux 1957–1977: 433.
6 Kroemer 2012: 55–92.
7 Nicholson 2001: 5.
8 *Si bona fuerit causa pugnantis, pugnae exitus malus esse non poterit, sicut nec bonus iudicabitur finis, ubi causa non bona, et intentio non recta praecesserit.* Bernard of Clairvaux 1963: 215.
9 *Ex cordis nempe affectu, non belli eventu, pensatur vel periculum, vel victoria christiani.* Bernard of Clairvaux 1963: 213.

10 Albert may have refused to participate in the eastern crusade because he wanted to defend his possessions from Henry the Lion, with whom he had an earlier conflict for the Saxon duchy.
11 Helmold of Bosau 1937: I, 88.
12 Wibald 1864: 245.
13 Sigebert of Gembloux 1844: 392.
14 The doctrine was highlighted by Pope Gelasius I (492–496) in his letters to the Roman Emperor Anastasius I. Morrall 1980: 22.
15 *Illud enim ommimodis interdicimus, ne qua ratione ineant foedum cum eis, neque pro pecunia, neque pro tributo.* Bernard of Clairvaux 1957–1977: 432.
16 *In variis autem expedicionibus, quas adhuc adolescens in Slaviam profectus exercuit, nulla de Christianitate fuit mentio, sed tantum de pecunia.* Helmold of Bosau 1937: I, 68.
17 *Sed quia Saxones potius pro auferenda eis terra, quam pro fide christiana confirmanda tantam moverant militiam.* Vincent of Prague 1861: 663.
18 Pertz 1859b: 82.
19 *Ad delendas penitus, aut certe convertendas nationes illas.* Bernard of Clairvaux 1957–1977: 432.
20 Jensen 2016: 233, Fonnesberg-Schmidt 2007: 32–33.
21 *Donec, auxiliante Deo, aut ritus ipse, aut natio deleatur.* Bernard of Clairvaux 1957–1977: 433.
22 Lotter 1989: 291–292.
23 Helmold of Bosau 1937: I, 58.
24 Helmold of Bosau 1937: I, 65.
25 Helmold of Bosau 1937: I, 57.
26 Helmold of Bosau 1937: I, 84.
27 Helmold of Bosau 1937: I, 57, 62.
28 Helmold of Bosau 1937: I, 71.
29 Helmold of Bosau 1937: I, 85.
30 Helmold of Bosau 1937: I, 87.
31 Saxo Grammaticus 2015: 14.39.25.
32 Saxo Grammaticus 2015: 14.1.6.
33 Saxo Grammaticus 2015: 14.39.47.
34 Saxo Grammaticus 2015: 14.39.28.
35 Helmold of Bosau 1937: I, 59.
36 Helmold of Bosau 1937: I, 62.
37 Helmold of Bosau 1937: I, 65, Pertz 1859b: 82.
38 *Cepitque dominari in universa terra Slavorum, succrescens sensim et invalescens.* Helmold of Bosau 1937: I, 68.
39 Helmold of Bosau 1937: I, 70.
40 *Filii enim Nicloti Pribizlavu atque Wertizlavus non contenti terra Kycinorum et Circipanorum aspirabant ad requirendam terram Obotritorum, quam dux eis abstulerant iure belli.* Helmold of Bosau 1937: I, 93.
41 Helmold of Bosau 1937: I, 69.
42 Eugene III 1902: col. 1203 (no. 166).

Crusade ideology and Bernard of Clairvaux 17

43 *Eos aut christiane religione subderet, aut Deo auxiliante omnino deleret.* Annales Magdeburgenses 1859: 188.
44 Fonnesberg-Schmidt 2007: 38–39.
45 Eugene III 1902: col. 1203 (no. 166). Anselm's diocese was in the Hevelli territory, so he could not be active there without a military support.
46 Wibald 1864: 243.
47 *Cui cum Friderieo episcopo Magdeburgensi et Anshelmo Havelburgense episcopo, accepta cruce, contra paganos versus aquilonem habitantes profecti sunt, et plures ad fidem christianam converterunt et baptisaverunt.* Chronica principum Saxoniae et monumenta Brandenburgensia 1880: 481.

References

Bernard of Clairvaux. 1957–1977. 'Letter 457'. In *Sancti Bernardi Opera*, eds. Jean Leclercq et al., Vol. 8. Rome: Editiones Cistercienses.
Bernard of Clairvaux. 1963. 'Liber ad milites Templi: De laude novae militae'. In *Sancti Bernardi Opera*, eds. Jean Leclercq, C. H. Talbot and Henri Rochais, Vol. 3. Rome: Editiones Cistercienses.
Bysted, Ane et al. 2012. *Jerusalem in the North: Denmark and the Baltic Crusades, 1100–1522*. Turnhout: Brepols.
Eugene III. 1902. *Epistolae et privilegia*, eds. Jacques-Paul Migne et al., PL, 180. Paris.
Fonnesberg-Schmidt, Iben. 2007. *The Popes and the Baltic Crusades: 1147–1254*. Leiden-Boston: Brill.
Gaposchkin, Cecilia. 2013. 'From Pilgrimage to Crusade: The Liturgy of Departure, 1095–1300'. *Speculum* 88/1: 44–91.
Helmold of Bosau. 1937. *Helmoldi presbyteri Bozoviensis Cronica Slavorum*, ed. Bernhard Schmeidler, MGH SRG. Hanover: Impensis Bibliopolii Hahniani.
Holder-Egger, Oswald (ed.). 1880. *Chronica principum Saxoniae et monumenta Brandenburgensia*, MGH SS 25. Hanover: Impensis Bibliopolii Hahniani.
Jensen, Kurt V. 2016. 'Holy War – Holy Wrath: Baltic Wars between Regulated Warfare and Total Annihilation around 1200'. In *Church and Belief in the Middle Ages: Popes, Saints, and Crusaders*, eds. Kirsi Salonen and Sari Katajala-Peltomaa, 227–250. Amsterdam: Amsterdam University Press.
Kroemer, James. 2012. 'Vanquish the Haughty and Spare the Subjected: A Study of Bernard of Clairvaux's Position on Muslims and Jews'. *Medieval Encounters* 18/1: 55–92.
Lotter, Friedrich. 1989. 'The Crusading Idea and the Conquest of the Region East of the Elbe'. In *Medieval Frontier Societies*, eds. Robert Bartlett and Angus MacKay, 267–307. Oxford: Oxford University Press.
Morrall, John B. 1980. *Political Thought in Medieval Times*. Toronto: University of Toronto Press.
Niall, Christie and Gerish, Deborah. 2003. 'Parallel Preachings: Urban II and al-Sulamī'. *Journal of the Medieval Mediterranean* 15/2: 139–148.

Nicholson, Helen. 2001. *Love, War, and the Grail: Templars, Hospitallers and Teutonic Knights in Medieval Epic and Romance, 1150–1500*. Leiden: Brill.
Pertz, G. H. (ed.). 1859a. *Annales Magdeburgenses*, MGH SS, 16. Hanover: Impensis Bibliopolii Hahniani.
Pertz, G. H. (ed.). 1859b. *Annales Palidenses*, MGH SS, 16. Hanover: Impensis Bibliopolii Hahniani.
Saxo Grammaticus. 2015. *Gesta Danorum: The History of the Danes*, ed. Karsten Friis Jensen, trans. Peter Fisher, 2 vols. Oxford: Oxford University Press.
Sigebert of Gembloux. 1844. *Sigeberti Gemblacensis chronica cum continuationibus*, ed. L. K. Bethmann, MGH, SS 6. Hanover: Impensis Bibliopolii Hahniani.
Vincent of Prague. 1861. *Vincenti Pragensis Annales*, ed. Wilhelm Wattenbach, MGH SS, 17, 658–683. Hanover: Impensis Bibliopolii Hahniani.
Wibald. 1864. Wibaldi epistolae. In *Monumenta Corbeiensia*, ed. P. Jaffé. Berlin.

3 Forced conversion and the new canon law (*ius novum*)

The contradictory concepts of conversion were much debated by historians. The German mission across the Elbe has been analyzed as an evolutionary process since 1930, when Herbert Achterberg introduced the terms *Wortmission* ("conversion by word") and *Tatmission* ("conversion by deed").[1] A third method which was identified later – *Schwertmission* ("conversion by sword") – has sparked many polemics among historians. The last term has been used to explain how the conversion of the Wends, Livonians and Prussians became, in Kahl's vision, the work of military orders.[2] Since 1984, when Benjamin Kedar published his book on *Crusade and Mission*, many scholars would agree that the two concepts – mission and crusade – were interconnected.[3] Regarding the Baltic Crusades, some historians still believe there was a transition during the twelfth century from a peaceful to a forced conversion. Others have suggested that missionaries and ecclesiastical authorities often accepted the use of force.[4] Recently, Kurt V. Jensen suggested that in some of the narrative sources for the Baltic Crusades written around 1200, there are two different attitudes to warfare. One attitude is that religious warfare should be regulated, limited and only used to protect missionaries and other Christians. This would enable missionaries to preach the Gospels to the pagans. The other was an exhortation to total war, in which conversion by preaching was much less important than physical annihilation of the pagans. The two approaches are seen as different aspects of the same discussion about religious warfare. Therefore the same writer could express both of these visions in the same text.[5]

For Christian authors like Adam of Bremen or Helmold of Bosau, the Wendish *ritus* was a mixture of religious and political apostasy, and some ancient beliefs. As long as their veneration did not involve subjection to ecclesiastical authorities, the Wendish idols might even be Christian saints. This idea was shared by Helmold of Bosau and Saxo

Grammaticus. Both were aware of the distinction between pagans and apostates. An example is the god Svantevit from Arkona, where he had a statue with four heads (polycephaly). The god was worshipped with offerings of cattle, wine and honey cakes the size of a man. Every year, the Rugians chose a Christian who was sacrificed in honour of the god. The offerings were received not only from Rugians, but from all Wendish tribes.[6] Originally, the cult of Svantevit was a Christian one. During the rule of the Frankish Emperor Louis the Pious (814–840), the Rugians were converted by the monks of the Benedictine monastery of Corvey. Later the Rugians would become apostates, worshiping St Vitus, the patron of the Corvey monastery, as a god.[7] Svantevit was worshipped not only by Rugians, but by Christians as well. The Danish King Sweyn III offered a chalice to the high priest of the temple in Arkona, which hosted Svantevit's statue.[8]

It is very likely that the conversion was a complex process that was influenced by several non-religious factors. The narrative sources show us the different types of conversion. From an individual to a collective conversion and supported by clergy or army, the mission must be understood as a social and political phenomenon, to which is added a cultural component. The pope or his emissaries could not exhort Christians to convert by sword a peaceful population which did not violate any treaties concluded with secular leaders. In most cases, the Church supported a forced conversion only against apostates. In this instance, the Wendish apostasy was both religious and political. It could be explained by the fact that the Wendish leaders made no distinction between secular and ecclesiastical subjection. Both the duke and the bishops were seen as greedy tyrants and criminals. The Danish Archbishop Absalon of Lund was described by Saxo Grammaticus as both cleric and warrior. He started his career not only as bishop, but also as a military leader with a glorious victory over the Rani. His actions are just because he is guided by wisdom and virtue. Unlike Valdemar I, who is hesitant and easy influenced by his people, Absalon is more confident and full of initiative. Absalon's physical involvement in the conflict was aimed at defending the Church against the Rugians. Saxo went further by considering the killing of Rugians a service equalling that of a priest celebrating the sacraments.[9]

In Saxony, only Henry the Lion had the right to appoint bishops in the dioceses across the Elbe. Therefore the bishops were seen as secular authorities under the jurisdiction of the Saxon duke. In some cases, the nobles could become bishops' vassals. Perhaps the best example is the count of Ratzeburg, Henry of Badewide, who became the vassal of Bishop Evermod of Ratzeburg. To show gratitude to the Saxon duke who appointed him, Henry of Badewide made a regular donation to the diocese of Ratzeburg. His example was followed by Count Adolf II of Holstein.[10]

It is possible that the ecclesiastical authorities collected not only the tithe but also the tribute. However, the heavy tribute to the Saxon nobles made them revolt and at the same time maintained hostility towards ecclesiastical authorities. The Wendish insurrections were illegal according to the previous tributary relations. For the Church, the insurrections were seen as a rejection of Christ. Therefore the Church had no choice but to follow the juridical arguments of the Saxon nobility. Of course, the juridical arguments were fully legitimate according to the Saxon nobility, but spiritually empty, so the Christian apologists had to fill that space with theological arguments.

Some of the twelfth-century apologists extended the concept of crusading. They argued that fighting for Christ against enemies such as apostates was meritorious in the sight of God and thus worthy of a spiritual reward proclaimed by the papacy, as the only legitimate authority. This is why the Wends were not seen by contemporaries as a peaceful population, but often as an *apostatica gens*. The tradition of forcing the Wends to return to Christianity goes back to the beginning of the eleventh century. In a letter to King Henry II (1002–1024), Bruno of Querfurt emphasized their forcible reconversion according to the principle *compellere intrare* that was applied only to apostates.[11]

The Wendish attacks during the eleventh century that led to the destruction of churches and the persecution of Christians had to be somehow punished in a just way. Central elements such as vengeance (*vindicta*, *ultio*), justice (*iustitia*), love (*ardor*, *caritas*) and zeal (*zelus*, *cupiditas*, *aviditas*) are often interconnected with crusading rhetoric. The strong connection between these emotional elements was emphasized by contemporary writers.[12] For Bernard of Clairvaux, zeal was a religious emotion connected to the desire to force heretics to convert. He approved of zeal as a central emotional impulse from God, but he rejected deeds without zeal. In his vision, faith should come as a suggestion powered by a just zeal, and not be enforced. Yet the human agents must "carry the sword" for a just cause. Otherwise, they could drag others into their error (Romans 13:4).[13]

Helmold of Bosau depicted less devotion among the crusader army that marched against the Wends in Dobin. The army was led by Henry the Lion and spiritually guided by Archbishop Adalbero of Hamburg-Bremen. A Danish army joined the army led by the Saxon duke. Saxo Grammaticus tells us that the Danish crusaders had the same status as the crusaders who fought in the Holy Land, and followed the same ritual practices as those who fought in Levant. By adopting "the emblems of the holy crusade" (*sacrae peregrinationis insignibus*), they made their war against the Wends as legitimate as that of the Crusaders in Levant. The term used by Saxo refers to the crusaders' oath about their intention of journeying to Jerusalem. This may refer to taking the cross or to the traditional attributes of a pilgrim.[14] Yet from Helmold's discourse we may observe that the main motivation for joining the crusade was religious zeal. The Saxons had gained zeal after they had been "signed with the sign of the cross" (*signo crucis insignita*).[15] In this way, he stated that the crusaders' goal was "to avenge the death and destruction that had been brought upon worshippers of Christ".[16] This hateful speech could be seen as a punishment for the killing of Christians. Prior to the Saxon invasion, Niklot had "secretly" invaded Liubice (Lübeck) and "slain there three hundred or more men". Among them were also clerics like the priest and monk Rotholph.[17] The Saxons' zeal was not always connected with anger, but also with devotion, mercy and love. Count Adolf, who would not have participated in the crusade, was zealous in ransoming the Danish captives held by Niklot.[18]

The emotional impulse had to come from the highest spiritual authority. The punishment of the Wends was seen as justice for the temporal power (e.g. Saxon nobles), which could regain political supremacy across the Elbe. This punishment would not exterminate the Wends, but it would have redressed the relationship with the ecclesiastical authorities. The Saxon punishment could be morally justified by Wendish inhumanity towards Christians. From a rebellious population, the Wends would become obedient. The Saxon nobles became the main protectors of the Christians across the Elbe. This measure facilitated the re-establishment of ecclesiastical authority. In *Annales Palidenses* we learn that the Saxons avenged atrocities committed by pagans against the Danish captives.[19] However, Henry the Lion did not have much interest in bringing the Wends back into the Christian fold. For him, their religious status was not so important. It was enough to receive the tribute from the Wendish leaders, who were free to follow their own religious option. This is why apologists such as Bernard of Clairvaux used theological arguments to convince their Saxon audience that a military campaign would bring not only the temporal subjection of the Wends, but also a spiritual integration within the Saxon *imperium Christianum* of Henry the Lion.

An idea based on divine vengeance has also been connected to our "pagan" Wends. The Saxon and Danish chroniclers were familiar with this idea, which applied in the case of apostates. A true crusader had to act under an emotional impulse, which was shared among other members of his communities (e.g. knights). Both chroniclers described emotions commonly shared by their contemporaries. A crusade could redirect violence from internal conflicts to external wars. In this way, a war against apostates could be justified in moral and legal terms. The Danish crusaders who fought against the Wends in 1147 were led by the two rival kings who concluded a truce (Sweyn III and Canute V). They refused to fight each other and marched against the Wends to "avenge the sacred things" (*sacrorum vindictam convertunt*).[20] Both the Saxon and the Danish crusaders were driven by an ardent desire for revenge.[21] In 1168, Valdemar I was "led by his eagerness to shed blood" during the siege of Arkona.[22] Apostasy could be a good reason for an invasion followed by a forced conversion. In the first decade of the twelfth century, the Polish King Bolesław III invaded Pomerania. Fearing that they would be slaughtered by the king, the inhabitants of the city of Alba (Białogard) surrendered.[23] Their prince, Gneuomir, accepted to be baptized with Bolesław as a godfather. Later, the Pomeranian prince rebelled against Bolesław. His conversion had not been valid because it was faithless.[24] This apostasy was seen in both religious and political terms and justified the next expeditions, which led to the conquest of the entire region. For Vincent of Cracow, these campaigns were acts of vengeance (*ultionem adiecit ultioni*) because the Pomeranians had not kept the true faith.[25] Only in this context was Bishop Otto of Bamberg able to perform his missionary journeys in Pomerania.

While a rebellious Christian might be physically coerced to adhere publicly to the Church, patristic texts emphasized that the key moment in a heathen's conversion to the Christian faith was the act of believing in the Christian God. Therefore this apostolic conversion should not be forced, but voluntary.[26] Since the time of Pope Gregory I (590–604), the Church had believed that no person was to be forced to become a Christian against his will.[27] Augustine of Hippo was a source of inspiration for many medieval theologians. During the twelfth century, forced conversion was condemned by canonists.[28] The ban was nuanced in various ways. One of the most conclusive examples is from Gratian, who became one of the most important canonists. His *Concordia discordantium canonum* (*c.* 1150), known more frequently as the *Decretum*, is considered a medieval handbook of canon law and perhaps the first comprehensive and systematic mixture of ecclesiastical writings on warfare and military matters. There, he emphasized that the Church should not convert infidels like Jews by force. Or at least, they should not be forced to believe without receiving willingly the grace of the Holy Spirit. Yet in *causae* 4 and 5, he stated that if a Jew was baptized by any kind of constraints against his will, then he could be considered a Christian and his baptism would be valid. However, this mention is not precise on what ceremony constituted a legitimate conversion. It only states that if a Jew had been forcibly converted and received the major sacraments, he could be coerced to remain Christian. This meant that Jews would not be converted by force but only through a sort of persuasion and by their free will. In this way, the grace of the Holy Spirit would have been received as an emotional impulse.[29]

Around 1164, Rufinus of Bologna discussed the issue of forced conversion. He made a distinction between absolute coercion, which was rejected, and conditional coercion, which was accepted. He referred to infidels, pagans and apostates without distinction. Yet he offered no clear guidance on where to draw the line between the two types of coercion for baptism and oath.[30] His vision was adopted and argued by other later canonists such as the Bishop of Ferrara, Huguccio. He highlighted the significance of the legal terms used in canon law. The importance of his work (*Summa*, *c*. 1188) consists in establishing the jurisprudential ground rules for defining the validity of baptism. There, we find out that the coercion on baptism could be absolute (*coactio absoluta*) or conditional (*coactio conditionalis*). In his vision, this distinction was clear and somehow involved free will. What made the difference was the person's consent to accept baptism. It did not matter how a person was coerced to accept baptism, provided he gave his consent, which was seen as a choice.[31] Thus absolute coercion could include any kind of physical or mental torture, but excluded the person's consent. On the other hand, a conditional coercion included both torture and consent. Huguccio agreed with conditional coercion because the person's consent could bring the grace of the Holy Spirit. If a person was forced to accept baptism without consent, baptism would not be valid.[32]

From a theological point of view, medieval Christians needed Jews, but they did not need Muslims and pagans. Since Augustine, Christians had used the Jews to remind themselves about the suffering of Christ. They were also useful to fulfil St Paul's prophecy that at the end of the world all Jews would recognize Christ and convert to Christianity by their own will. This eschatological vision did not apply to other infidels. In the context of crusade ideology, Islam was, on the other hand, Christianity's main military and religious opponent. As for the Wends, military power and the importance of conversion were emphasized by indirect association with Muslims. In Bernard's letter, they were not named, to emphasize the irrelevance of ethnic details in this universal struggle between good and evil. The Wends had to be seen by the Saxons as the main military and religious opponents, just like

Muslims by Christians in the East. The crusading ideology preached by apologists like Bernard influenced the Saxon vision. From regional enemies that deserved punishment for not paying tribute, the Wends had been integrated into a religious war on a global scale. The key component of the mechanism was forced conversion.

Even if it was forbidden by the canon law and theology, forced conversion was a method of subduing some populations considered pagan or apostate. Few examples of forced conversion were to be encountered from the eighth century onwards. In the following centuries, it was the expression of secular power and functioned together with the missionary idea promoted by the local ecclesiastical authorities. Charlemagne's intention to subdue the Saxons is based on a form of political and religious apostasy.[33] Their forced conversion took place within a legal framework. For Charlemagne, the Saxons had no choice but to accept baptism "preached with the iron tongue" (*ferrea quodammodo lingua praedicavit*). In his eyes, the resistance of Saxons who had undergone baptism and signed a treaty of allegiance amounted to political high treason and religious apostasy.[34] Yet if the wars of conversion were contrary to canon law, the popes, and later crusading preachers, were often tempted to present their audience with what they wanted to hear.

The idea of forced conversion as an expression of the legitimacy of a dynasty also inspired the Ottonians.[35] In this case, the Saxons had a long tradition of wars of conversion from the perspective of both victim[36] and oppressor. Later, the forced conversion became useful to the leaders of the First Crusade as well as the Saxon nobility. In his speech at Clermont, Pope Urban II combined the concept of kingship with canon law and theology. Urban defined the portrait of an ideal monarch who had to respond to the divine call. Robert the Monk, who wrote one of several Latin histories of the First Crusade, noted that at Clermont Urban remembered the forced baptism of the Saxons ordered by Charlemagne. The pope motivated his French audience, referring to the greatness of Charlemagne and representing the French, as the descendants of the Franks had who destroyed the pagan kingdoms.[37] From the time of the Second Crusade, the idea of converting pagans or bringing back apostates into the Christian fold began to take root as a motivation for religious warfare. The Wends were perhaps one of the best examples of forced conversion. This vision was shared by contemporary writers. In a continuation of the chronicle of Sigebert of Gembloux, written at Anchin abbey in northern France (*Auctarium Aquicinense*), we find that the Saxon and Danish crusaders forced the Wends to accept Christianity.[38]

Notes

1 Achterberg 1930: 87.
2 Kahl 1955: 363–370, Ekdahl 1989: 205–206, Hellmann 1985: 65, Boockmann 1981: 108–110, Ščavinskas 2014: 499–527.
3 Kedar 1984.
4 Fonnesberg-Schmidt 2007: 74.
5 Jensen, Kurt V. 2016: 228–229.
6 Saxo Grammaticus 2015: 14.39.8.
7 Helmold of Bosau 1937: I, 6, 52; II, 108 and Saxo Grammaticus 2015: 14.39.13.
8 Jensen, Carsten S. 2017: 159. For more details about the cult of Svantevit, see Zaroff 2002: 9–18.
9 For more details regarding the clerical involvement in war against the pagans in the Baltic region, see Jensen 2017: 405–406.
10 Helmold of Bosau 1937: I, 77.
11 For more details regarding the Wendish apostasy at the beginning of the eleventh century, see Kahl 1955.
12 The idea of a divine retribution that became human justice in the Wendish Crusade of 1147 has been discussed at more length by Dragnea 2016: 49–82, here 50.
13 Bernard of Clairvaux 1958: 186–187.
14 Gładysz 2012: 70.
15 *Festinavit omnis illa expedicio signo crucis insignita… zelare iniquitatem ipsorum*. Helmold of Bosau 1937: I, 65.
16 *Ulturi mortes et exterminia, quae intulerunt Christicolis*. Helmold of Bosau 1937: I, 62.
17 Helmold of Bosau 1937: I, 63.
18 Helmold of Bosau 1937: I, 66.
19 Pertz 1859: 82.
20 Saxo Grammaticus 2015: 14.3.5.
21 Saxo Grammaticus 2015: 14.3.6.
22 Saxo Grammaticus 2015: 14.39.2.
23 Vincent Kadlubek 1892: III, 2, 2–6.
24 *Talium fides sit ipsa perfidia*. Vincent Kadlubek 1892: III, 5, 1.
25 Vincent Kadlubek 1892: III, 14, 1.
26 A relevant example is the hagiographer Ebo, which stated that the Pomeranians' adherence to Christianity in Otto's (Otto of Bamberg) missions was a voluntary one. *Non vult Deus coacta servicia sed voluntaria*. Ebbo 1869: III, 6.
27 Muldoon 1979: 11.
28 Kedar 1984: 73–74.
29 Gratian 1959: D 45, c 4, c 5.
30 Rufinus of Bologna 1963: c. 22, q. 5, c. 1.
31 *De coactione autem distinquo, aut est absoluta aut est conditionalis. Si absoluta coactione quis baptizetur, puta unus tenet eum ligatum et alius*

superfundit aquam, nisi (ubi Lons-le-Saunier*) postea consentiat, non debet cogi ad fidem Christianam tenendam.* Huguccio 1916: 16, no. 1.

32 *Si vero coactione conditionali quis baptizetur, puta: te verberabo vel spoliabo bel interficiam vel ledam, nisi baptizeris, debet cogi ut fiedm teneat, quia per talem coactionem de nolente efficitur quid volens, et volens baptizatur. Voluntas enim coacta voluntas est et volentem facit.* Huguccio 1916: 16, no. 1.

33 The Saxon apostasy was highlighted in *Annales Laureshamenses* as follows: *Quasi canis revertit ad vomitum suum, sic reversi sunt ad paganismum quem pridem respuerant, ... conati sunt in primis rebellare contra Deum, deinde contra regem et christianos; omnes ecclesias que in finibus eorum errant, cum destructione et incendio vastabant, reiicientes episcopos et presbyteros qui super eos erant, et aliquos comprehenderunt, nec non et alios occiderunt, et plenissime se ad culturam idolorum converterunt.* See Pertz 1829: 792, 45.

34 For more details about the forced conversion in the Baltic area, see Dragnea 2016: 65–71.

35 The forced conversion of the Saxons by Charlemagne was discussed in Kedar 1984: 68 and Becher 2013: 23–52.

36 Not only the Saxon clergy were victims of the Wendish insurrections, but also Danes such as the missionary dean Oddar, a member of King Svend's family, who was killed by the Wagri in Oldenburg during the insurrection that took place in 1018. Jensen, Kurt V. 2017: 66.

37 Strack 2012: 35–36.

38 *Daci et Westphali ac Saxonum duces consenserunt in hoc, ut aliis euntibus Ierosolimam contra Sarracenos, ipsi viciam sibi Sclavorum gentem aut omnio delerent aut cogerent christianam fieri.* Sigebert of Gembloux 1844: 392.

References

Achterberg, Herbert. 1930. *Interpretatio Christiana: Verkleidete Glaubensgestalten der Germanen auf deutschem Boden*. Leipzig: H. Eichblatt.

Becher, Matthias. 2013. 'Der Prediger mit eiserner Zunge. Die Unterwerfung und Christianisierung der Sachsen durch Karl den Großen'. In *Schwertmission*, eds. Hermann Kamp and Martin Kroker, 23–52. Paderborn: Schöningh.

Bernard of Clairvaux. 1958. 'Sermones super Cantica Canticorum'. In *Sancti Bernardi Opera Omnia*, eds. J. Leclercq and H. M. Rochais, Vol. 2. Rome: Editiones Cistercienses.

Boockmann, Hartmut. 1981. *Der Deutsche Orden: Zwölf Kapitel aus seiner Geschichte*. München: Beck.

Dragnea, Mihai. 2016. 'Divine Vengeance and Human Justice in the Wendish Crusade of 1147'. *Collegium Medievale* 29: 49–82.

Ebbo. 1869. *Ebbonis vita Ottonis episcopi Bambergensis*, ed. Philip Jaffe, BRG, 10. Berlin: Weidmann.

Ekdahl, Sven. 1989. 'Die Rolle der Ritterorden bei der Christianisierung der Liven und Letten'. In *Gli inizi del Cristianesimo in Livonia-Lettonia*, 203–243. Rome: Libreria Editrice Vaticana.

Fonnesberg-Schmidt, Iben. 2007. *The Popes and the Baltic Crusades: 1147–1254*. Leiden and Boston: Brill.
Gratian. 1959. *Decretum magistri Gratiani*, ed. Aemilius Friedberg, CIC, 1. Graz: Akademische Druck- und Verlagsanstalt.
Gładysz, Mikołaj. 2012. *The Forgotten Crusaders: Poland and the Crusader Movement in the Twelfth and Thirteenth Centuries*. Leiden: Brill.
Hellmann, Manfred. 1985. 'Altlivland und das Reich'. In *Felder und Vorfelder russischer Geschichte: Studien zu Ehren von Peter Scheibert*, eds. I. Auerbach, A. Hillgruber and G. Schramm, 61–75. Freiburg: Rombach.
Helmold of Bosau. 1937. Helmoldi presbyteri Bozoviensis Cronica Slavorum, ed. Bernhard Schmeidler, MGH SRG. Hanover: Impensis Bibliopolii Hahniani.
Huguccio. 1916. *Summa ad*, D. 45 c.5, v, *associatos unctos corporis Domini*, Admont Stiftsbibliothek, MS 7, fol. 61va–b. Quoted by F. Gillmann, *Die Notwendigkeit der Intention auf Seiten des Spenders und des Empfängers der Sakramente nach den Anschauungen der Frühscholastik*. Mainz: Kirchheim.
Jensen, Carsten S. 2017. 'Bishops and Abbots at War: Some Aspects of Clerical Involvement in Warfare in Twelfth- and Early Thirteenth-Century Livonia and Estonia'. In *Between Sword and Prayer: Warfare and Medieval Clergy in Cultural Perspective*, eds. Radosław Kotecki, Jacek Maciejewski and John Ott, 404–434. Leiden: Brill.
Jensen, Kurt V. 2016. 'Holy War – Holy Wrath: Baltic Wars between regulated Warfare and Total Annihilation around 1200'. In *Church and Belief in the Middle Ages: Popes, Saints, and Crusaders*, eds. Kirsi Salonen and Sari Katajala-Peltomaa, 227–250. Amsterdam: Amsterdam University Press.
Jensen, Kurt V. 2017. *Crusading at the Edges of Europe: Denmark and Portugal c.1000–c.1250*. London and New York: Routledge.
Kahl, Hans-Dietrich. 1955. 'Compellere intrare: Die Wendenpolitik Bruns von Querfurt im Lichte hochmittelalterlichen Missions- und Völkerrechts'. *Zeitschrift für Ostforschung* 4: 161–193, 360–401.
Kedar, Benjamin Z. 1984. *Crusade and Mission: European Approaches toward the Muslims*. Princeton: Princeton University Press.
Muldoon, James. 1979. *Popes, Lawyers, and Infidels: The Church and the Non-Christian World, 1250–1550*. Philadelphia: University of Pennsylvania Press.
Pertz, Georg H. 1829. *Annales Laureshamenses*, MGH SS 1. Hanover: Impensis Bibliopolii Hahniani.
Pertz, G. H. (ed.). 1859. *Annales Palidenses*, MGH SS, 16. Hanover: Impensis Bibliopolii Hahniani.
Rufinus of Bologna. 1963. *Summa Decretorum*, ed. H. Singer. Aalen: Scientia.
Saxo Grammaticus. 2015. *Gesta Danorum: The History of the Danes*, ed. Karsten Friis Jensen, trans. Peter Fisher, 2 vols. Oxford: Oxford University Press.
Sigebert of Gembloux. 1844. *Sigeberti Gemblacensis chronica cum continuationibus*, ed. L. K. Bethmann, MGH, SS 6. Hanover: Impensis Bibliopolii Hahniani.

Strack, Georg. 2012. 'The Sermon of Urban II in Clermont and the Tradition of Papal Oratory'. *Medieval Sermon Studies* 56: 30–45.
Ščavinskas, Marius. 2014. 'On the Crusades and Coercive Missions in the Baltic Region in the Mid-12th Century and Early 13th Century: The Cases of the Wends and Livonians'. *Zeitschrift für Ostmitteleuropa-Forschung* 63/4: 499–527.
Vincent Kadlubek. 1892. *Ex magistri Vincentii Chronica Polonorum*, ed. Max Perlbach, MGH SS, 29. Hanover: Impensis Bibliopolii Hahniani.
Zaroff, Roman. 2002. 'The Origins of Sventovit of Rügen'. *Studia Mythologica Slavica* 5: 9–18.

4 The conquest of a pagan territory blessed by the Church

The emergence of the crusade phenomenon influenced missionary traditions in northern Europe. Thus the prospect of forced conversion was intertwined with the concepts of crusade and mission. The validity of forced conversion is dealt with almost exclusively in writings influenced by canon law. According to late Roman theological tradition going back to Augustine, the use of force to achieve religious aims was justified only if the enemy of the Church proved to be an obstinate heretic. Emotional impulses played an important role in Augustine's rhetoric. For him, the love of a sinner could legitimize his punishment through war. This meant that a just war could be seen as a charitable act that brings spiritual benefits. However, his texts on "just war" (*bellum iustum*) were "rediscovered" at the end of the eleventh century, when Bishop Anselm of Lucca included them in his *Collectio canonum*.[1] The presence of these canonical writings in the papal letters, sermons, chronicles and other sources related to crusades is quite low.[2]

From Carolingian times to the mid-eleventh century, the papacy was unable to resolve on a concept of war. The popes could launch a war against anyone who opposed their policies. Things began to change only during the reign of Pope Leo IX (1049–1054). Through his reformist spirit, Leo extended the concept by using biblical images to show the juridical influence of Augustinian thinking. Leo believed that divine vengeance against the enemies of the papacy could be accomplished only by Christians who were obedient to Rome. That is why Leo called martyrs all those who died at Civitate in 1053, fighting on his side against the Normans.[3] In this context a new institution would appear, which distinguished the crusades from the previous "holy wars". Thus the evolution of the *bellum iustum* doctrine made the papacy allow the use of force in order to regain the heretics and apostates.[4]

From the second quarter of the eleventh century, disobedience to royal authority as well as to the papacy was often seen as a step towards idolatry and heresy. The idea of a divine vengeance that had become human justice was popular among clerics such as Anselm in Canterbury, who in *Cur Deus Homo*, written during the last decade of the eleventh century, highlighted a new theory of divine vengeance. According to this theory, disobedience to secular and ecclesiastical hierarchical structures attracted divine punishment. A worldly alternative was the satisfaction of an insult and the rank of the person insulted, in order to maintain a balance within the social order. Thus Anselm developed a sort of theory of divine vengeance within the Church's penitential system. Satisfaction of insult became a sort of currency that could be used to attain one's moral due. In a dialogue with his students, Anselm used Pauline rhetoric (Romans 12:19) when he claimed that vengeance is the work of God, whose anger can become human justice.[5]

Augustine's *bellum iustum* was interpreted by other canonists in various forms. Gratian emphasized that the love of a person could legitimize his punishment through a just war. If the sins were evil, the love was sacred. The love was seen as an emotional impulse coming from God. Thus what was moral and pleasant to God was considered legal. Of course, the ultimate authority was God Himself and his punishment became a divine vengeance.[6] Those who served in a just war would not be considered criminals, because they fought with the right authority. They could be seen as moral agents like modern vigilantes. In this way, the punishment applied to a sinner would have prevented him from committing other sins. An example given by Gratian is the mutilation of pirates or thieves.[7]

This struggle between moral agents and evil forces was seen as a holy war. Humans were the instruments of God's wrath. His orders were received through emotional impulses. When they acted under His command, they responded to a moral duty. Their actions were not condemned by the Church, but rather blessed. It is very likely that other clerics such as Helmold of Bosau shared similar thinking. The moral justification of the Wendish Crusade was interconnected with the juridical and was sought in the Old Testament books of the Maccabees. The memory of the Maccabees and other Old Testament quotations played an important role in shaping the idea of crusading and its migration to new frontiers in the Baltic and Iberia. In the two books of Maccabees we have a pattern in the wars fought by the Maccabees in the name of God against his unbelieving enemies (1 Maccabees 15:33). Therefore these books seemed very usable for the moral justification of wars against the Wends.[8] Within a biblical framework, Helmold of Bosau compared the Wends with the Amorites. The latter were defeated by the Maccabees and the Israelites (the Saxons) as a result of a divine vengeance.[9] For

Helmold, the conflicts between Christian Saxons and apostate Wends became a sort of "sacred history". The imitation of the Old Testament battles of Israel against idolatry rendered the Saxon struggle legitimate in the eyes of the clergy. This would have emphasized the idea that the conquest of the Wendish territories by the Saxons was as legitimate as that of the Crusaders in the Levant.

A war against a pagan population could be justified if it had the purpose of protecting missionaries, new converts and churches. In this case, knights were called to rise up against the Wends. Canon law fully accepted this type of war, especially when aimed against those pagan leaders who might forbid any missionaries from entering their lands to preach the Gospels. However, the moral justification was a complex process and certainly not an easy task for later theologians. According to Augustinian thinking, a *bellum iustum* could aim at reconquest and defence rather than conquest and forced conversion. Originally, the forced conversion of infidels formed no part of crusader ideology. Even if the Wendish territory had a Christian ecclesiastical organization for a short time, it was not considered to be integrated into the Christian world like any other German province. Therefore, organizing a crusade at the edges of Christian Europe called for the construction of a moral and legal basis. The arguments of this complex mechanism were mainly theological, described against a juridical background. The papacy, as the only legitimate authority, could declare a war, but only if it had to serve a *causa iusta*.

To bring this mechanism into motion, it was necessary for the Wendish territory to become sacred. This would have worked in an analogy with the Holy Land. The first and the most important connection with the Holy Land was made in the so-called "Magdeburg letter", which was written in the first decade of the twelfth century. The anonymous author is believed to have been a Flemish cleric, perhaps from the entourage of Archbishop Adelgot of Magdeburg. As we know, the letter is an appeal for help against the Wends and it seems to have been addressed to the clergy of Saxony, Rhineland and Flanders and princes such as Robert of Flanders who had participated in the First Crusade with great success. The letter was not a true crusading document, but it shows how crusading ideas were assimilated within the Saxon ecclesiastical authorities. The author of the letter described the Wendish insurrections against the Saxon secular and ecclesiastical authorities as evil. The profanation of churches and the slaughter of Christians made them "the most cruel gentiles" and "men without mercy". Among these atrocities, the author emphasized the scalping and ritual decapitation of Christians, whose heads were offered as sacrifices to the Wendish gods. When he mentioned the Wendish raids, the author stated that they took place *in nostram regionem*, without specifying the exact location. What we know is that the invaded territories were Christian (*christianorum fines*).[10]

It is very likely that the territory to which the author of the letter refers was that of the Obotrite state, where until 1066 there was an ecclesiastical organization. At that time, the Wagrians and the Obotrites were led by Prince Gottschalk, a good Christian and probably for a short time a faithful tributary of the Saxon Duke Bernard II. The prince was educated in the Saxon monastery of the Billung family in Lüneburg. Thus the central event in the Magdeburg letter is the Wendish insurrection of 1066 against Gottschalk and the Saxon ecclesiastical authorities. Adam of Bremen tells us that in the context of this insurrection the Redari, one of the rebel groups, celebrated in Rethra the ritual decapitation of the captured Bishop John of Mecklenburg, whose head, stuck on a lance, was given to their god, Riedegost.[11] The killing of Gottschalk, the most enthusiastic supporter of the Saxon ecclesiastical authorities across the Elbe, was seen as an attack against Christendom.

In order to justify the conquest of the lost territory, the author of the letter uses the rhetoric of the First Crusade. Even if the atrocities committed by the Wends are highlighted, they are not directly associated with those of the Muslims in the Levant. Yet the cruelty of the Wends requires a punishment equal to the crusaders' bravery and sacrifice in the Holy Land. The only direct association was made between the Christian territory across the Elbe and Jerusalem. Therefore all Christians are invited to liberate the Wendish territory, which is called *Hierusalem nostra*, "as did the men of Gaul for the liberation of Jerusalem" in Levant.[12]

Jerusalem was seen not only as an idea or a place, but also as a physical manifestation of holiness. Thus Christians in the north tried to transfer the symbol of Jerusalem to the periphery of Christendom.[13] The newly converted territory of the Wends was made sacred following the model of the Holy Land. It became a small copy of Jerusalem. This meant that a conquest would be legitimate if followed an emotional impulse like the crusader zeal in the Holy Land. From a worldly regional conflict, which was based mostly on material interests, the conflict with the Wends has thus become a holy war between good and evil. The author offered no indulgences, which were papal privileges. Yet the only spiritual reward offered in the letter is the salvation of the soul, which is connected with the acquisition of land. Thus the prospect of obtaining lands was an additional inducement, which often helped to intensify the crusader's zeal. It was emphasized that this promise of a double reward was adopted from Robert the Monk and originates from the Bible (Matthew 19:29; Exodus 3:8).[14] In a similar way, the author invited all "Saxons, French, Lorrainers and Flemings, most renowned and conquerors of the world" to "acquire the best land in which to live", which is "rich in meat, honey, corn and birds".[15]

What we may notice is that for the author, the idea of pilgrimage implies not the journey (*iter*) or expedition (*expeditio*) to holy places, which did not exist across the Elbe, but only the concept of holy war and colonization. His audience is made up of a kind of *peregrini* who create sacred places only by conquering and protecting them. An interesting thing is that the author does not omit the Saxons (both warriors and clergy), who are mentioned first among the guest list. This meant that the archbishop of Magdeburg recognized the Saxon Duke Lothair of Supplinburg (king from 1125, emperor from 1133), as the first legitimate authority to conquer and protect the Wendish territory. However, the religious authority which initiated the call came from the archbishop of the Saxon archdiocese of Magdeburg, who supported King Henry V (emperor from 1111) during the final phase of the Investiture Controversy. The same order also appears in the exhortation to the clergy to preach the so-called crusade which, however, did not take place. Thus all "bishops, clerks and monks" from Saxony, France, Lorraine and Flanders were urged to spread the call in "churches and all dioceses and parishes".[16]

About a century after the Magdeburg letter was written, Bishop Vincent of Cracow made a direct association between a pagan population in the Baltic region and Muslims. In the context of the foundation and consolidation of Poland, he described the battles of Piasts with Hungarians, Bohemians and Germans as well as the pagan Pomeranians and Prussians across the Baltic coast. Some of these military expeditions were described as holy wars aimed at converting the pagans or getting apostates back into Christendom. The moral justification for these campaigns was not an easy task. It included mostly theological arguments. In Vincent's vision, the pagans who had received baptism by force are obliged to abide by it. A forced conversion had to be avoided because it could become a religious and political apostasy. If they were not Christian, the use of force was not pleasing to God.[17] Therefore the expeditions organized by the Piasts were seen as a result of individual decisions that did not always follow the divine will. The fate of a battle could have been decided by both wrong emotions (greed, hate) and immoral actions (sins). Vincent saw the expeditions of Bolesław III against the Pomeranians (1109), Bolesław IV to Prussia (1147, 1166), and Casimir I against the Sudovians (1191–1192) as crusading campaigns. What is even more interesting in Vincent's discourse is that he described the Prussians as "the enemies of the faith" and *Saladinistas*.[18] This obvious reference to infidels and their Sultan Saladin (1174–1193) allows us to understand the complex dimension of crusading ideology at the beginning of the thirteenth century. The Polish battles against the pagan Prussians seen as the kinsmen of Saladin are part of the same holy and just war which from the second half of the twelfth century can be waged anywhere on earth. Prussians are dangerous to the Polish state and Piasts as Saladin, "the most obstinate enemy of the Holy Sepulchre", was to the Kingdom of Jerusalem and Christians. Thus the expedition against the Prussians is described as being as worthy as any crusade to the Holy Land.[19]

The first part of Vincent's work may be based on a previous Polish chronicle from *c.* 1115, called *Gesta Principum Polonorum*. The author, known as Gallus Anonymus, suggested that the expeditions of the Polish Duke Bolesław III against the Pomeranians were just wars because they were a response to Pomeranian raids into Poland. The author emphasized the religious and political apostasy of Pomeranians and the attempts of the Polish dukes to maintain Christianity among them:

> On the northern Sea, [Poland] has as neighbors three most savage nations of pagan barbarians, Selencia, Pomerania, and Prussia, and the duke of the Poles is constantly at war with these countries, fighting to convert them to the faith. But neither has the sword of preaching been able to sway their hearts from faithlessness, nor the sword at their throats wipe out this generation of vipers in its entirety. Yet often their leaders when defeated in battle by the Polish duke have taken refuge in baptism, only to deny the Christian faith when they recovered their strength and take up arms afresh against the Christians.
>
> (Gallus Anonymus 2003: I, Prohem, 12)

Since he attended the Fourth Lateran Council in 1215, Bishop Vincent was well informed about the contemporary vision of religious warfare. His discourse reflects the hope and faith that secular leaders have put into religious-military orders. The Bishop was very skilful in choosing his words regarding the Polish wars in Prussia. In a similar manner to Bernard, Vincent tried to justify the Polish right to conquer Prussia with theological arguments. What we know is that Vincent is the first example of a direct association between a pagan population in the Baltic region and Muslims. Both groups seems to share the same status in the hierarchy of the enemies of Christ. The Prussians are no longer those barbarian neighbours, dangerous only for their incursions into Poland. By the first decade of the thirteenth century, they have become stronger, and the Polish kingdom was fragmented. In 1209 Pope Innocent III authorized the Cistercian monk Christian of Oliva to convert the Prussians. The Duchy of Masovia ruled by Conrad I, and especially the region of Kulmerland, became the object of constant raids by Prussians who refused to pay tribute to the Polish duke. In response, Conrad called on the pope for help several times. In order to secure the protection of the Christians, together with the first Bishop of Prussia, Christian of Oliva, Conrad founded a local militia which in 1228 became the Order of Dobrin (Dobrzyń) or *Fratres Milites Christi de Prussia*.[20] The Order of Dobrin did not have enough knights so Conrad summoned the Teutonic Order for help. In 1228, the Teutonic Knights arrived in Prussia, where they engaged in fighting with the Prussians to prevent their incursions into Kulmerland. In 1235, the majority of the Knights of Dobrin joined the Teutonic Order, as allowed by a papal document known as the *Golden Bull of Rieti*.[21]

Notes

1 For more details regarding the canon laws assembled by Anselm of Lucca in the context of the Gregorian Reform, see Cushing 1998: 64–102.
2 Tyerman 2006: 47.
3 Bull and Housley 2003: 178.
4 John Gilchrist believes that the doctrine of *bellum iustum* only took shape in Carolingian times. In previous centuries, the Church forbade clergy to use weapons and imposed penance on soldiers who were killing their enemies in battle. For more details about the evolution of the *bellum iustum* doctrine, see Gilchrist 1988: 174–197, Claster 2009: 36–37, Mastnak 2002: 1–90, Bliese 1991: 1–26, Russell 1977: 16–39.
5 *Nulla in hoc est repugnantia, quia deus hoc nobis praecipit, ut non praesumamus quod solius dei est. Ad nullum enim pertinet vindictam facere, nisi ad illum qui dominus est omnium; Nam cum terrenae potestates hoc recte faciunt, ipse facit, a quo ad hoc ipsum sunt ordinatae.* Anselm of Canterbury 1895: I, 12.
6 *Vindicta, que ad correctionem ualet, non est prohibenda.* Gratian 1959: C 23, q 4.
7 Gratian 1959: C 23, q 3, c 6.
8 The Maccabean ideas in sources concerning the early Crusades and divine vengeance were analyzed in Morton 2010: 275–293.
9 Helmold of Bosau 1937: I, 22, 34. 64.
10 In this paper I used the original text in Latin. *Epistola pro auxilio adversus paganos (Slavos)*, 625 and the English translation by Riley-Smith J. and Riley-Smith L. 1981: 75.
11 Adam of Bremen 1876: III, 50.

12 *Erumpite et venite omnes amatores Christi et ecclesie et sicut Galli ad liberationem Ierusalem vos preparate! Hierusalem nostra, ab initio libera, gentilium crudelitate facta est ancilla. Epistola pro auxilio adversus paganos (Slavos)*, 625.
13 For more details about the symbolism of Jerusalem in the Baltic region and Iberian Peninsula, see Jensen 2016: 153–176.
14 Lotter 1989: 276.
15 *Sed terra eorum optima carne, melle,... farina, avibus et, si excolatur, omnium de terre ubertate proventuum [referta], ita ut nulla ei possit comparari. Sic aiunt illi, quibus nota est. Quapropter, o Saxones, Franci, Lutharingi, Flandrigene famosissimi et domitores mundi, hic poteritis et animas vestras salvifacere et, si ita placet, optimam terram ad inhabitandum acquirere. Epistola pro auxilio adversus paganos (Slavos)*, 626.
16 *Itaque, fratres charissimi, totius Saxonie, Francie, Lutaringie, Flandrie episcopi, clerici et monachi, de bonis sumite exemplum et Gallorum imitatores in hoc etiam estote, clamate hoc in ecclesiis, sanctificate ieiunium, vocate coetum, congregate populum, annunciate hoc et auditum facite in omnibus terminis prelationis vestre! Epistola pro auxilio adversus paganos (Slavos)*, 626.
17 Vincent Kadlubek 1892: III, 12, 1.
18 Vincent Kadlubek 1892: IV, 16, 19.
19 Güttner-Sporzyński 2015: 64.
20 Boas 2016: 151.
21 For more details regarding the conquest of Prussia under the Teutonic Order, see Leighton 2018: 457–483.

References

Adam of Bremen. 1876. *Adami gesta Hammaburgensis ecclesiae pontificum*, ed. J. M. Lappenberg, MGH SRG. Hanover: Impensis Bibliopolii Hahniani.
Anselm of Canterbury. 1895. *Cur Deus Homo*. London: David Nutt.
Boas, Adrian J. 2016. *The Crusader World*. London and New York: Routledge.
Bliese, John R. E. 1991. 'The Just War as Concept and Motive in the Central Middle Ages'. *Medievalia et Humanistica* 17: 1–26.
Bull, Marcus and Housley, Norman (eds.). 2003. *The Experience of Crusading. Volume One: Western Approaches*. Cambridge: Cambridge University Press.
Claster, Jill N. 2009. *Sacred Violence: The European Crusades to the Middle East, 1095–1396*. Toronto: University of Toronto Press.
Cushing, Kathleen G. 1998. *Papacy and Law in the Gregorian Revolution: The Canonistic Work of Anselm of Lucca*. Oxford: Oxford University Press.
Gallus, Anonymus. 2003. *Gesta Principum Polonorum*, eds. Paul W. Knoll and Frank Schaer. Budapest and New York: CEU Press.
Gilchrist, John. 1988. 'The Papacy and War against the "Saracens", 795–1216'. *The International History Review* 10/2: 174–197.

Gratian. 1959. *Decretum magistri Gratiani*, ed. Aemilius Friedberg, CIC, 1. Graz: Akademische Druck- und Verlagsanstalt.

Güttner-Sporzyński, Darius von. 2015. 'Constructing Memory: Holy War in the Chronicle of the Poles by Bishop Vincentius of Cracow'. In *Crusades and Memory: Rethinking Past and Present*, eds. Megan Cassidy-Welch and Anne E. Lester, 51–66. London and New York: Routledge.

Helmold of Bosau. 1937. *Helmoldi presbyteri Bozoviensis Cronica Slavorum*, ed. Bernhard Schmeidler, MGH SRG. Hanover: Impensis Bibliopolii Hahniani.

Jensen, Kurt V. 2016. 'Crusading at the End of the World: The Spread of the Idea of Jerusalem after 1099 to the Baltic Sea Area and to the Iberian Peninsula'. In *Crusading on the Edge: Ideas and Practice of Crusading in Iberia and the Baltic Region, 1100–1500*, 153–176. Turnhout: Brepols.

Leighton, Gregory. 2018. 'Did the Teutonic Order Create a Sacred Landscape in Thirteenth-century Prussia?' *Journal of Medieval History* 44/4: 457–483.

Lotter, Friedrich. 1989. 'The Crusading Idea and the Conquest of the Region East of the Elbe'. In *Medieval Frontier Societies*, eds. Robert Bartlett and Angus MacKay, 267–307. Oxford: Oxford University Press.

Mastnak, Tomaž. 2002. *Crusading Peace: Christendom, the Muslim World, and Western Political Order*. Berkeley: University of California Press.

Morton, Nicholas. 2010. 'The Defence of the Holy Land and the Memory of the Maccabees'. *Journal of Medieval History* 36: 275–293.

Riley-Smith, Jonathan and Riley-Smith, Louise. 1981. *The Crusades: Idea and Reality*. London: E. Arnold.

Russell, Frederick H. 1977. *The Just War in the Middle Ages*. Cambridge: Cambridge University Press.

Tyerman, Christopher. 2006. *God's War: A New History of the Crusades*. Cambridge, MA: Harvard University Press.

Vincent Kadlubek. 1892. *Ex magistri Vincentii Chronica Polonorum*, ed. Max Perlbach, MGH SS, 29. Hanover: Impensis Bibliopolii Hahniani.

Wattenbach, Wilhelm. 1882. 'Epistola pro auxilio adversus paganos (Slavos), "Handschriftliches"'. In *Neues Archiv*, 7, 625.

5 Expanding the crusading ideal on the eastern shore of the Baltic

In the last decades of the twelfth century, theology was reinterpreted by canonists and commentators close to the papacy, such as Enrico, Cardinal of Ostia, or the bishop of Ferrara, Huguccio. They shared a new moral and juridical conception of war, which allowed knights the right to fight against the enemies from inside and outside the Church. All those foes usurped territories legally owned or claimed by Christians under the "law of nations" (*ius gentium*) and the "divine law" (*Divina lex*). The war against unbelievers was considered illegitimate when it was used to convert or exterminate them. The *bellum sacrum* began to be studied by canonists only in the thirteenth century. For canonists of the thirteenth century such as Cardinal Enrico, all those who did not recognize the pope's authority were perceived as rebellious in both moral and legal aspects. They did not have permission to hold any titles and rights and therefore needed to be subdued.[1]

Appearing in the crusading context and influenced by the concept of German kingship, the idea of forced conversion as a reaction to political and religious apostasy spread over the Baltic region. The Danish expeditions against the Wends from 1147 onwards made Denmark a regional power, later recognized by the Holy Roman Emperor Frederick II. From the end of the twelfth century, when the conflicts with the Wends ended, the Danish kings started to increase their interest in the eastern Baltic region. Their involvement in military campaigns against the Wends was reduced to forced conversion.[2] In Estonia, along with the Danish knights, there were also preachers. The first mission in Estonia took place in the time of Archbishop Eskil of Lund, Absalon's predecessor. The mission was possible thanks to the efforts of the Danish secular powers, who sought to ensure ecclesiastical independence from the archdiocese of Hamburg-Bremen. In 1104 the Archdiocese of Lund was founded, responsible for the whole of Scandinavia, and thus the Danish Church became independent from Germany.[3] Eskil was described as a very pious man and always zealous for the welfare of the Church. He was well known for his vigorous promotion of monasticism in Scandinavia and intention to reform Danish church law. His education started at the cathedral school of Hildesheim. Eskil enjoyed a close friendship with Bernard of Clairvaux and other great prelates of his time. He managed to create an impressive network of friends, especially from the circles of Bernard of Clairvaux, Pope Alexander III, Archbishop Thomas Becket of Canterbury and the abbot of St Remi at Reims, Peter of Celle. His missionary idea in Estonia may have occurred at the suggestion of Bernard, whom he met in 1150 at the Clairvaux abbey.[4] It is very likely that the missionary activity in Estonia was supported by the Cistercian Order. The Cistercians came to Denmark and Sweden through the intervention of Eskil. The establishment of the Cistercian Order in Scandinavia took place after the Synod of Lund in 1139. There, Eskil proposed to all the Scandinavian ecclesiastical authorities to allow the Cistercians to establish abbeys in Scandinavia. Therefore, the first Cistercian abbeys in Scandinavia were founded in 1143 (Sweden), 1144 (Denmark) and 1146 (Norway).[5]

Absalon proved to be very much in the style of his predecessor. He zealously patronized the Cistercian order and supported the conversion of the Estonians. However, the Danish interest in organizing missions in Estonia is mentioned in one letter of Peter of Celle, written to Eskil between 1172 and 1174. Peter was close to Eskil. The two were the central figures behind the missionary plan for Estonia. The abbot of St Remi was both the initiator and the supporter of the mission, which was sponsored and coordinated by Eskil.[6]

The idea of converting the Estonians in some ways followed the Bernardine model applied across the Elbe. The mission could have been threatened by the Estonians, and in this case, a crusade would become necessary. In a letter sent to Eskil's successor, Archbishop Absalon, Peter expressed his concern regarding possible retaliation against Eskil's family, accused of rebellion against the Danish King Valdemar I. Peter also reminded Absalon of the great missionary work of his predecessor, which he needed to continue.[7] The conflict between Eskil and Valdemar started because along with Frederick I, the Danish king supported the antipope Victor IV against Pope Alexander III (1159–1181). On the other hand, Alexander III was supported by Eskil. In 1156, Pope Adrian IV (1154–1159) made him a papal legate, in order to ensure the independence of the Scandinavian churches from German imperial dominance. Another reason behind the conflict with Valdemar was the royal appointment of bishops. The right to appoint bishops was a power-control tool, because it could prevent the prelates from falling into the hands of the competing party. A good example is Eskil, who for his anti-royal attitude can be compared with Thomas Becket. However, his exile is linked to the incident mentioned above, which was resolved only after the reconciliation between Valdemar and Alexander in 1170. At the same time, Eskil fulfilled the papal wish to canonize the king's murdered father, Prince Canute Lavard, the first duke of Schleswig and vassal of King Lothair of Supplinburg. The infant Canute, King Valdemar's eldest son, was crowned by Eskil as co-regent of Denmark with his father. The event is important in Danish political history because it consolidated the rule of Valdemar and his successors as well as their triumph against the ecclesiastical power. In 1177, Pope Alexander III accepted Absalon, a supporter of Valdemar, as the new archbishop of Lund. Soon after this event, Eskil decided to resign and move to France. Five years later he died at Clairvaux abbey.[8] Absalon, Valdemar's right-hand man, who was already Bishop of Roskilde, refused to accept the election. Saxo Grammaticus tells us that Eskil fixed this issue by releasing all his knights from their oath of fealty and made them swear a new oath (*militiae fides*) to Absalon.[9]

This action could be seen as a transfer of ecclesiastical authority. Alexander accepted the appointment of Absalon as Archbishop of Lund, but could not guarantee ecclesiastical authority among a divided clergy. It is very likely that at least some Danish prelates and most of the clergy were followers of Eskil in his conflict with Waldemar. After all, Eskil was driven by a strong religious fervour and was thus the right person to reform the Danish Church. Yet the idea of reforming the Church under the impulse of religious orders had as its main obstacle the royal power. The reconciliation between the Danish king and the pope could not definitively erase the previous conflicts and pave the way for religious reformation.

However, placing knights under the command of Absalon must be seen in the context of the evolution of the doctrine of the holy war. The involvement of the two prelates in the campaigns of conquest and conversion of the Rugians shows us that they were aware of the need for military support in the mission. After the Estonians were subjugated, the missionaries benefited from military assistance. It is very likely that Absalon took the same aggressive attitude against the Estonians. Absalon's crusading fervour won him the approval of the Cistercians, who saw the crusade as an opportunity to save souls through conversion, and not as a moral and legal justification for a conquest. The missionaries who preached in Estonia would be protected by his knights. Missionaries would request protection from Estonians who did not accept baptism and would put their lives in danger. Therefore as in the

Wendish case, the acceptance of baptism was a consequence of physical constraint, and not a voluntary act.

During his exile, Eskil was hosted in Rheims by Peter of Celle, with whom he planned the mission in Estonia. The mission was to be carried out by a Benedictine monk named Fulco, brought from the abbey of Montier-la-Celle and consecrated as Bishop of the Estonians by Eskil. We do not know in which context Fulco was elected to spread Christianity in Estonia. It is generally assumed that he was French, perhaps a trusted friend or even a relative of Peter. This explains why Abbot Peter sent letters of recommendation to the pope for Fulco and why he urged Eskil to support the missionary work financially. Peter must have been sufficiently convincing, for Pope Alexander agreed to support Fulco's mission. His interest was highlighted by three letters written in September 1171 or 1172 at Tusculum. The letters confirm that Peter acted as an intermediary between Eskil and the papacy. In one of the letters, Alexander asked Archbishop Eystein of Nidaros (Trondheim) to assign an Estonian monk named Nicolaus to assist Fulco.[10] No further information survives about Fulco's mission in Estonia and the conversion methods he used there. It is very likely that Fulco's preaching among the Estonians was spread through Nicolaus, a native speaker of Estonian. Since Fulco was most likely French, preaching in Estonian by a local cleric would provide not only a faster and easier conversion, but also the ecclesiastical authority for the Scandinavian Church. This is not a singular case. There are other examples when the Gospel was spread through local clerics who preached in a language other than Latin. Even if he is considered to have known Polish, in his missions in Western Pomerania, Otto of Bamberg was assisted by Polish clerics such as the Archbishop of Gniezno, Jakub of Żnin, Bishop Aleksander of Płock, Chancellor Michał Adwaniec and the chaplain of Bolesław III, Wojciech (Adalbert), who became the Bishop of Cammin.[11]

However, after some delay, Fulco was ready to make his journey in the north. It was assumed that Fulco was active in Estonia between 1172 and 1177 and returned to France one year after Eskil had resigned his office and retired to Clairvaux.[12] This might suggest that Fulco's mission depended upon Eskil's ecclesiastical authority and his military and financial support. This is confirmed by another letter, in which Alexander urged the Danes to make material donations to support Fulco's mission.[13] However, Fulco's missionary experience is confirmed by another letter issued in 1180 by Pope Alexander. In the letter it was stated that Fulco was one of the main actors regarding the "protection and growth of the Christian faith" in Rügen and its incorporation in the diocese of Roskilde.[14]

Alexander III is the first pope known to have paid direct attention to missionary war as well as crusade in Estonia and Finland. He may have sent Fulco to convert the Finns as soon as his assistant Nicolaus could take over the missionary work among the Estonians. However, there is no mention of an ecclesiastical authority in Finland under Folquinus, a semi-mythical bishop who came from Sweden.[15] Fulco's importance in the Estonian mission is highlighted by Alexander in a letter issued in September 1171 or 1172 at Tusculum. In the letter, Alexander exhorted the Scandinavian kings and princes and other faithful Christians not only to defend, but also to extend the Christian faith in Estonia. The crusade was to be a reaction to the suffering of the Christian community in Estonia, where the local population allegedly harassed priests. The expedition was morally and legally justified by the savagery of the Estonians and their attacks. The pope highlighted the Estonians' rebellious character. He specifically mentioned that their attacks are an act of rebellion against both the ecclesiastical and the secular authorities. Therefore the letter can be seen as an authorization to all Scandinavian kings to conquer and convert the Estonians and other pagan neighbours. The participants benefited from the forgiveness of sins for one year, just like those who visited the Church of the Holy Sepulchre in Jerusalem. Those who died in the battle could receive forgiveness of all sins if they did penance.[16] However, we do not know how the Scandinavian kings and princes reacted to Alexander's exhortation to crusade. His call received no written answer. This could be explained by the fact that Fulco was sent to Denmark by Peter of Celle not earlier than 1174. We do not know if Fulco arrived in Estonia before or after his departure for Denmark. Indeed, Fulco's journey to Denmark was prepared by Alexander in September 1171 or 1172. In a letter written in 1172 or 1173, Peter of Celle informs the King of Sweden, the Swedish nobility and the Archbishop of Uppsala that Fulco has postponed his journey in the north owing to a flood and in order to assist him during his visit to Rome.[17] Yet in another letter of Peter of Celle to Absalon issued between 1178 and 1180, we learn of Fulco's presence in Denmark in the archbishop's entourage.[18]

Alexander did not follow Eugene III's line regarding the indulgences offered to the crusaders who fought in Estonia. The Saxons who marched against the Wends received a plenary indulgence. The Saxon armies were led by many German prelates, some invested with the authority of papal legates. Yet Alexander did not give the participants a plenary indulgence, nor even temporal privileges given those who fought in the Holy Land. For Alexander, the crusade against the Estonians had a different character from the crusades in the Holy Land. It aimed to

44 *Expanding the crusading ideal*

justify the conquest of a pagan territory. Conversion was seen as a consequence of the conquest. Alexander's vision was influenced by the fear of a repeat of the events of the Second Crusade, when the diffusion of material resources over three different theatres of war had led to military failure and lowered morale in the whole of Western Christendom. It seems that Alexander created a hierarchy of penitential war in the service of the Church, in which the crusaders in Iberia and the Baltic region were rewarded with partial indulgences. This action limited the pope's control in these regions. Therefore the Baltic crusades were supported rather by archbishops and bishops than by the papacy and the Scandinavian kings and princes.[19]

The moral and legal justifications of penitential war in the Baltic region varied according to political context. The papacy had to respond to petitions from both secular leaders and clergy, who were already involved in various military campaigns as well as missionary activity. Both Eugene III and Alexander III allowed the forced conversion of the pagans, which directly contradicted the canonists before the twelfth century. Unlike Eugene, Alexander highlighted the defence of Christendom from pagan attacks. Celestine III (1191–1198) allowed the use of force against the apostates in Livonia, in order to bring them back into the Christian fold.

The first major Danish expeditions in Estonia took place during the reign of King Canute VI (1182–1202). Saxo Grammaticus tells us that in 1184, the king authorized a full-scale naval expedition against the pagan Estonians. The expedition was organized by the zealous inhabitants of Scania and Sjælland, who missed the religious wars of Valdemar's time.[20] Their emotional impulse was given by a few previous Estonian and Kurs (Couronian) pirate attacks that threatened Danish trade in the Baltic sea.[21] The effectiveness of pagan attacks and their naval fleet (e.g. Öselians from Saaremaa island, neighbours to the Kurs) is confirmed by the *Livonian Rhymed Chronicle*,[22] a Middle High German verse history composed around 1290. The chronicle reveals a contemporary interpretation of Christian chivalry, and the institutional ideals of Teutonic Order military monasticism.[23]

That Danish campaigns in Estonia had the character of a crusade was highlighted by Henry of Livonia. In a similar manner to the conquest of Rugia by his father, in 1206 the Danish King Valdemar II (1202–1241) gathered a large army, with which he marched in Saaremaa. Henry declared that the Danish crusaders were fired by the zeal of vengeance as they sought to subject the Öselians and other pagans to the Christian faith.[24] The Öselians were not a single case of forced conversion. The *Livonian Rhymed Chronicle* gives us information about the religious wars fought by the Danish crusaders against the Couronians. Their stubbornness in refusing baptism led to a major military confrontation and cost the lives of many of them. Finally, constrained by the Danish knights, the Couronians accepted Christian baptism.[25]

Unlike the conquest of Rugia, Absalon did not participate in the campaigns in Estonia. The absence of any mention of Absalon's involvement in the Estonians' conversion could be related to the fact that the archbishop wanted to secure his archdiocese. Saxo emphasized Absalon's political and military activities in a striking contrast with the previous Danish bishops. Unlike his predecessor Eskil, and his successor Anders Sunesen (1201–1228), Absalon showed an interest in strengthening the position of his archdiocese and the rulership of the Danish king. This was achieved by increasing the wealth of the suffragan dioceses and the public revenue. The situation led to massive Danish revolts. Saxo Grammaticus tells us that the Danes from Scania had revolted against the collectors of the public revenue. The revolt could not be stopped even after Absalon had gone to Scania and publicly addressed "the hostile assembly with greater frankness than persuasiveness".[26]

It was very probably Eskil who introduced the two concepts of mission and crusade to Denmark. He acted as the primate of the Danish and Swedish Churches and also as a papal legate for Scandinavia. Thus the archdiocese of Uppsala was subordinated to the Danish archdiocese of Lund, headed by Eskil. Previously, in 1156, Pope Adrian IV had given Eskil the authority to create an independent Swedish archdiocese. This happened only in 1164, when a Cistercian monk known as Stefan, from the Swedish abbey of Alvastra, was consecrated by Eskil as the first archbishop of Uppsala. The ceremony took place in Burgundy in the cathedral of Sens in the presence of Pope Alexander III.[27]

In his intention to convert the Estonians, Eskil acted as a politician. His ecclesiastical interests were mixed with secular ones. Important support came from the Swedish king, who at that time was on good terms with the papacy. The acknowledgment of the Swedish king's authority over ecclesiastical organization is confirmed by Pope Alexander III in a letter addressed to King Karl Sverkersson (1161–1167). The letter highlighted the double monarchy of Karl, called an "illustrious king", who ruled over all the bishops and counts in the kingdom of *Svear* and *Götar*. Karl adopted the title used by Alexander in most of the royal documents which he signed.[28] Pope Innocent III also enjoyed good relations with the Swedish monarchy, supporting the future King Sverker II (1196–1208), son of Karl, in his struggle with Erik X (1208–1216).[29]

46 *Expanding the crusading ideal*

Among those who sailed on the eastern shore of the Baltic were also Norwegians. The kings and nobles of Norway were interested in organizing military expeditions in Estonia. In the Icelandic *Sverris saga*, we find out that Prince Eirik Sigurdson, brother of the King of Norway, Sverre (1184–1202), led a "voyage" in Läänema (western Estonia). The Norwegian fleet had five ships and one of them was led by a certain Ozur Perst, probably a cleric. We do not know in which year the expedition took place nor if it was organized perhaps in a joint action with the Danish King Canute VI. We only know that the ships sailed in the summer of the years 1185–1188, and that the Norwegian knights "plundered heathen lands".[30]

Pope Innocent III (1198–1216) showed an interest in the crusade in both theory and practice. Only seven months after he became pope, Innocent issued the encyclical *Post miserabile* proclaiming the Fourth Crusade (1202–1204) and calling upon the West to take up arms against the Muslims. Thus European kings and princes were urged to liberate Jerusalem and to avenge the wounds inflicted on Christians. Innocent believed that the Muslim occupation of the Holy Land was a shame to the whole of Christendom, because in that region Christ died for the salvation of all men.[31] The Fourth Crusade ended with the conquest of Constantinople and the establishment of the Latin Empire in April 1204. The original plans of the papacy were not achieved, which is why in May 1208, Innocent tried to recruit a crusading army in France, and on December the same year issued another encyclical, *Utinam dominus*. Here, the pope claimed the support of the Lombard League and the March of Ancona for a crusade in the Holy Land.[32] However, the desired support did not come, forcing the pope to issue in April 1213 a new encyclical, *Quia major*. This time, Innocent stated that the participation in the Fifth Crusade (1213–1221) was an obligation for Christians. Therefore the idea of penance had a secondary importance.[33] This situation modified the rhetoric of the crusade, and as a result, the prominent role of the Cistercians was taken over by the new mendicant orders (*Ordines mendicantes*).[34] Extensive preparations for the Fifth Crusade were only made at the Fourt Lateran Council of 1215.[35]

Meanwhile, Innocent expressed his interest in the integration of the eastern Baltic regions into Christianity. He did not refer only to pagans from Livonia, but also to other schismatics like Russians. The first connection between Livonia and Rus' dates from the pontificate of his predecessor, and took place in the context of the appointment of Livonia's first bishop, Meinhard of Üxküll (1188–1196). Innocent's interest in the integration of the Russians within Western Christianity is highlighted in his correspondence with the third Livonian bishop, Albert.[36] The election of a third bishop in Livonia in a short time was related to the failure of previous conversion missions from the time of Meinhard and Berthold of Hanover (1197–1198). Around 1180 Meinhard, a regular canon at the Segeberg abbey in Holstein, settled on the river Daugava at Üxküll (Ikšķile). In the following years he built a stone church there, dedicated to Our Lady. At that time, the pagan Livonians were tributaries of Prince Vladimir Vseslavich of Polotsk (1186–1215). Therefore the conversion of the "the idolatrous Livonians" was possible only with the permission of the prince.[37] The mission was supported by Archbishop Hartwig II of Hamburg-Bremen (1185–1207), who in 1186 consecrated Meinhard as bishop of Üxküll. More than that, Hartwig was able to obtain the support of Pope Clement III (1187–1191). In 1188, the pope confirmed Hamburg-Bremen's metropolitan rights over the diocese of Üxküll, and the consecration of Meinhard as bishop for this see.[38] It is very likely that the idea of the mission belonged to Hartwig, whose archdiocese had a long tradition of supporting the conversion of the pagans in the north. Furthermore, this measure was in accordance with papal mission policy from the twelfth century onwards. Thus the initiative and responsibility for missionary activity lay with local archbishops and bishops. The popes merely blessed the conversion and authorized the mission by appointing papal legates.

Meinhard came from Segeberg, where there was a very active missionary community led by Bishop Vicelin of Oldenburg (1149–1154). Vicelin's missionary work entered deeply into the memory of generations of Segeberg missionary clerics. Among them was the young Meinhard, whom he may even have known personally. Meinhard adopted the Augustinian rule for the new church in Üxküll and soon began to preach in Livonia as Vicelin did in Holstein. Meinhard had a broader view of the recruitment of field missionaries. He did not restrict the mission to the Augustinian rule, but also admitted members of other orders as participants in the mission. Thus Meinhard was assisted by some German merchants and Cistercian monks who travelled to Livonia. Among the Cistercians was Theodoric from the abbey of Loccum, who, according to Henry of Livonia, organized a mission in Treyden (north of Üxküll).[39] Meinhard initially converted most of the Livonians, but, faced with resistance and apostasy, he turned to the idea of a crusade. He was aware of the possibility that apostasy might spread. Like the spiritual leaders of the Wendish Crusade of 1147, he understood that both the acceptance of baptism and the maintenance of Christianity required military assistance. Therefore after experiencing the Livonian apostasy, in 1196, Meinhard sent a messenger to ask the pope's advice. The chronicler Henry of Livonia tells us that the pope was aware that the spread of apostasy would lead to the loss of control over Livonia. Celestine believed that the Livonians should be forced to keep their promises (e.g. acceptance of baptism) and not to repudiate the Christian faith. If they were able to persuade the Livonians to maintain Christianity, the crusaders would benefit from the remission of all sins.[40]

Celestine did not try to justify the crusade as Eugene III had done in 1147 with the Wends. There are no mentions of attacks on Christians or the destruction of churches. The pope's intention was to sacralize a territory on the periphery of Christendom. Therefore the motivation that inflamed the crusaders was regaining control of a territory that was Christian. For his successors, Livonia was considered a new "promised land", a worthy destination for pilgrimage, which would be transformed into a domain of the Mother of God (*Terra Mariana*).[41]

Meinhard's successor, Berthold, was abbot of the Cistercian monastery of Loccum in Hanover. It is very likely that he assisted Meinhard in his missions in Livonia. After he became a bishop in 1197, Berthold continued Meinhard's mission plan of gaining confidence and goodwill by kindness. At first the Livonians appeared to become less hostile, but soon their old hatred of the Saxon ecclesiastical authorities revived. Berthold's advantage was that he could benefit from the fortifications built along the river Daugava by his predecessor (e.g. at Üxküll and Holm). Within the fortifications, Christians held their religious services and could protect themselves from the Livonian attacks. Unlike his predecessor, Berthold did not succeed in converting the Livonians. He therefore also approached the pope to obtain support for the mission. Henry of Livonia tells us that the pope's feedback was positive. He urged the Christians to take the cross and fight against the "perfidious Livonians". As before, he granted remission of sins to all participants.[42] Berthold was the spiritual leader of the Saxon crusader army that marched into Livonia in 1198. His intention was to compel the Livonians who accepted baptism to return to the Christian faith. The Livonian leaders allowed Berthold to convert their subjects only through preaching, and not by using force. However, peaceful conversion was impossible. During an unexpected battle, the bishop was killed by the Livonians. Fearing Saxon reprisals, a large number of Livonians accepted baptism. Besides this, every priest received a measure of grain from each plough.[43]

The year after Berthold's death, Archbishop Hartwig consecrated his nephew, Albert of Buxhövden, a canon from Bremen, as bishop of Riga. He was the third bishop of Livonia, ruling the diocese until his death in 1229. Henry of Livonia tells us that in 1201, Albert moved the convent of regulars and the episcopal see from Üxküll to the new city of Riga which was built in the same year. The episcopal cathedral and the entire region of Livonia were dedicated to Mary, the Mother of God.[44] As for the missionary activity, Albert learned from the mistakes of his predecessors. The hostility of the Livonians made him choose the sword instead of preaching. Forced conversion became a motivation for a crusade which was followed by a military conquest. This was possible with the help of the Livonian Brothers of the Sword (*Fratres militiae Christi Livoniae*), a military order established in 1202 by Albert or by the Cistercian missionary monk, Theodoric of Treyden.[45] As Henry of Livonia stated in his *Chronicon*, the major role of the Order was to provide military assistance to the bishop of Riga. Pope Innocent III sanctioned the Order. Thus he gave the Sword Brothers the rule of the Templars and also a badge on their clothing, in which a cross and a sword appeared.[46] The composition of the order was exclusively German. One of the hardest measures was to maintain the new conquests under German rule. A key person was Albert, who travelled annually to Saxony to recruit more crusaders. Albert also had to provide financial support for the Sword Brothers.[47] About Albert we know that he went on a recruitment campaign in Scandinavia and Saxony after his consecration in 1199. From Gotland he recruited about 500 men who took the cross and fought in Livonia. In Denmark he received gifts from King Canute VI, Duke Waldemar (the future King Valdemar II) and Archbishop Absalon of Lund.[48] In Magdeburg, at Christmas in the same year, Albert met the new German King Philip of Swabia (1198–1208), who helped him to recruit new armed pilgrims. Thus the "pilgrims" who took the cross and marched to Livonia were placed under the protection of the pope, who granted them the same plenary remission of sins as those who journeyed to Jerusalem.[49]

Albert re-established a missionary base at the mouth of the river Daugava, near the future city of Riga. The location of the new city was chosen for its commercial potential; the port could be easily transited by German and Scandinavian merchant ships. Riga became a privileged city only after the intervention of Innocent III, who urged merchants to use Riga instead of other cities in Livonia. From Saxony, Albert recruited not only soldiers, but also clerks, businessmen, craftsmen, shopkeepers and publicans, together with their families.[50] At the beginning of the thirteenth century, the urban elite in Livonia immigrated mostly from German lands. A small number of Livonians were also integrated into the emerging merchant class that temporarily or permanently settled in Riga, Tallinn, Tartu or other cities in Livonia. However, the Livonian merchants developed into a distinct professional and social group only after the crusades.[51] All these German-speaking colonists provided a Christian identity to the city, which was still surrounded by a hostile pagan population. Both the Livonians who were converted and a few other pagans were brought into the city. Most of the pagan Livonians were separated from the rest of the city, living outside its walls.[52]

The German colonists altered the cultural landscape of Livonia. Even if Latin became the main language used by the nobles and clergy for writing official documents and chronicles, the Livonians adopted a German lifestyle. It is more likely that those who facilitated the conversion of Livonia were mainly the clerics recruited by Albert. It has been pointed out that the methods used by these clerics followed the patterns of predecessors such as the seventh-century bishops St Eligius of Noyon and Amandus of Tongeren-Maastricht. The two prelates are well known for organizing missions in Flanders.[53]

Innocent's interest concerning the conversion of Livonia was most likely a reaction to the political context, and not a well-defined missionary strategy. Of course, the pope often spoke of the conversion. To be sure, his first reaction to Albert's missionary initiatives was limited to preaching and came only after 1204. Yet it was only after this year that the use of force for defensive purposes was accepted.[54] Most likely, as history shows us in the Wendish case, the conversion of the Livonians was stimulated by the Saxon and Scandinavian princes, and not by the papacy.

Henry of Livonia understood that the conversion missions organized under Albert's co-ordination followed the pattern of a recent missionary tradition, described by Adam of Bremen and Helmold of Bosau. The mass conversion of the Livonians took place after a local leader named Caupo was baptized by the Cistercian monk Theodoric of Treyden. After he accepted Christian baptism, Caupo, who is called "a sort of a king and elder" of the Livonians (*quasi rex et senior*) by the chronicler Henry, became a supporter of Albert's missionary policy. Like the Obotrite Christian rulers Gottschalk and Pribislav, Caupo was a defender of Christianity among his subjects. However, his connection to Christianity had a diplomatic side which the Wendish leaders did not have. Thus in 1203, at Albert's suggestion, Caupo travelled to Rome together with Theodoric, who introduced him to Innocent. The pope was interested in the religious status of other tribes outside Livonia that were probably not under Caupo's leadership. Henry of Livonia tells us that the pope received Caupo with gratitude, kissed him and gave many thanks to God for the conversion of his subjects.[55]

Caupo's visit to Rome could be connected with Albert's intention to bring the Sword Brothers under his control. From the foundation of the Order, the undisciplined Sword Brothers tended to ignore their supposed vassalage to Albert. In 1218, Albert asked Valdemar II for assistance, but the Danish king instead arranged a deal with the Master of the Order and conquered northern Estonia. For Albert, the Livonian leader was evidence for the feasibility of his missionary project. In Saxony, Albert lacked support from the ecclesiastical authorities. Archbishop Gerhard of Hamburg-Bremen (1219–1258) restricted the preaching of the continuous crusade in Livonia and forbade the recruitment of armed pilgrims from Lübeck.[56] Furthermore, in 1217, Pope Honorius III (1216–1227) placed the episcopal see of Riga under the auspices of Magdeburg instead of Hamburg-Bremen.[57]

Albert hoped that Caupo's visit to Rome would give credibility to his missionary project. Moreover, Innocent might persuade Gerard to support Albert with new recruits and perhaps money. However, what Innocent did was to give an exhortation and some instructions for the missionaries. Albert would have sent reports to the papacy in order to obtain any kind of support. Unfortunately, the reports have not survived, which prevents us from knowing how the case was presented by the Livonian ecclesiastical petitioners. In a letter issued on 5 October 1199 (*Sicut ecclesiastice religionis*) to the Christians of Saxony, Westphalia and the territory across the Elbe, Innocent refers to Albert's first reports to Rome. The letter, which is considered the first to the Livonian mission, can help us to understand the moral justification for the previous military campaigns and the use of force against pagans. The pope urged all Christians from the territories mentioned to assemble an army to aid the Christians in Livonia, who, after Bishop Meinhard's death, were under attack from the local pagan population. Unlike his predecessors, Innocent highlighted the killing of Christians as a moral justification for the conquest of Livonia, but not the conversion of the Livonians. Thus the armed pilgrims are invited to compel the unfaithful Livonians to enter into Christendom. Indirectly, the pope rebuked Albert for the previous mission wars. Perhaps, in his letters to Rome, Albert tried to associate crusade with pilgrimage by presenting the Saxon military campaigns in Livonia as similar to the crusades in the Holy Land. The pope was not convinced and therefore considered that the Livonians must accept the faith voluntarily, and not by force. He did not say by what means the knights could have compelled the Livonians to accept baptism. He only tried to describe the Livonian warfare in more canonically correct terms.[58]

Caupo was considered by the chronicler Henry of Livonia "the most faithful" (*fidelissimus factus est*) among Livonians. The epithet could be explained by the fact that after returning from Rome, together with the Christians, Caupo persecuted some of his pagan subjects and perhaps other neighbouring tribes. Therefore, in order not to be killed by them, he lived in Riga among the Christians for almost a year.[59] Henry also tells us that after his death in a crusade against the pagan Estonians which took place in 1217, Caupo left all his wealth to the churches of Livonia. Bishop Albert and other clerks from Riga mourned his death. However, Caupo did not have a genuine Christian funeral. His body was cremated and his bones were placed in a burial mound at Cubbesele (Sigulda).[60]

It was emphasized that Innocent III saw the conversion of the Livonians as a traditional missionary project, on the pattern established by Pope Gregory I.[61] Thus he believed that the conversion of Livonia had to be accomplished only through preaching and the voluntary acceptance of baptism. His letters contain few biblical passages. In a letter issued on 19 April 1201 (*Is qui ecclesiam suam*), Innocent offers advice on a number of issues such as the canonical regulation concerning marriage and consanguinity of the newly converted Livonians. The pope also reminds missionaries of their duty to preach, pointing to a so-called peaceful conversion.[62] The pope's exhortation contains quotes from the Gospel of Matthew referring to preaching, voluntary baptism and Christian obedience.[63] The "Parable of the Workers in the Vineyard" is compared with missionary work, and the "harvest" is a spiritual one.[64]

Innocent's view regarding the conversion of Livonia can also be seen from the narratives of Henry regarding Caupo's visit to Rome. Before his departure to northern Germany, from where he sailed to Riga, besides blessings and thanks, Caupo received from Innocent a hundred gold pieces as a gift for his support in the mission. To Bishop Albert, Innocent sent a Bible written by Pope Gregory I.[65] The Bible was offered through Theodoric, a well-known missionary, and not by Caupo. This gesture shows how the pope saw the conversion process. Indeed, he realized that the ecclesiastical authorities in Livonia needed the support of local elites. Even if he accepted baptism, Caupo was seen as a faithful supporter of the mission, who brought peace to Livonia, rather than a good Christian. Caupo's funeral ritual (cremation) could suggest that both he and perhaps the Livonian elites practised a type of religious syncretism. That is to say, Caupo understood the mission only in political terms, and not according to the missionary tradition in the Baltic region. That is how the pope's gesture of choosing Theodoric as a messenger can be explained. His missionary activity as well as his Cistercian background may have recommended him for this role.

The choice of a manuscript associated with Pope Gregory I shows that Innocent saw the mission in Livonia as being inspired by the apostolic conversion. At the end of the sixth century, Gregory I sent a mission to Britain under the coordination of the first Archbishop of Canterbury, Augustine. The missionaries, who had an intellectual background and a moral education, performed great deeds and many members of Anglo-Saxon elites were baptized.[66] The elites who converted to Christianity allowed the missionaries to preach freely. This is why the Gregorian model was followed by other popes such as Innocent III.[67] A relevant example is the eleventh-century bishop Otto of Bamberg, who, according to the hagiographers Ebo and Herbord, followed the Gregorian model. The idea is confirmed by a German manuscript from the Michelsberg abbey written in the first half of the twelfth century.[68] In the manuscript there is a miniature (Msc. Patr. 76) which was apparently added later. The miniature shows Bishop Otto holding a book with the inscription *Pastoralis cura*, recalling Gregory I's treatise of the same title.[69]

Innocent approved the use of force only for the purpose of defending missionaries and new converts. In a letter issued in October 1204 (*Etsi verba evangelizantium*), Innocent highlighted the existence of two distinct groups whose task was the conversion of the Livonians. The first group was exclusively ecclesiastical and included Cistercians, Benedictines and Canons Regular, who worked together for the mission. The second group was more heterogeneous, consisting of knights and any other laymen prepared to defend the "plantation" of the Christian faith against the "barbarians" threatening to destroy it. However, the conjuncture led to the organization in 1202 of the second group in a military order, which would become the Livonian Brothers of the Sword or simply Sword Brothers.

The arrival of crusaders from the German Crusade of 1197 onwards and the foundation of the Livonian Brothers of the Sword provided two new forms of armed support. This was enhanced by the bishop's secular vassals, and also by the new converts, who were forced to provide military service as a condition of acceptance as Christians. Yet the increasing deployment of Christian military force provoked hostile reactions from the pagan Livonians, who feared the loss of their political independence. Christians often raided Livonian territory. Besides seizing livestock, the Christians took captives to serve as slaves. In some cases, the Christian army besieged the fortifications of Livonian leaders, where their subjects frequently sheltered. The war in Livonia was designed to compel the pagan leaders to accept baptism and the ecclesiastical authorities in Riga. Thus under Bishop Albert, the mission became increasingly aggressive and this situation had to be known by the papacy.

Innocent's perception regarding the conversion of Livonia by preaching was highlighted in his letter issued in 1205 to the clergy of the Latin Patriarchate of Constantinople (*Evangelica docente Scriptura*). In the letter, the pope suggested that unification of the two Christian churches could take place in a peaceful way. As an example, Innocent mentioned the conversion of the Livonians through preaching. The submission of the Orthodox clergy to the Catholic faith would be voluntary, as with the acceptance of baptism by the Livonians. Therefore the inclussion of Greeks, Vlachs, Bulgarians or other "schismatics" would be peaceful, and not a consequence of the conquest of Constantinople in 1204.[70] For Innocent's successors, the defence of Latin Constantinople was an essential condition for the liberation of Jerusalem, to which the crusaders would have to march through Byzantine territory. All the popes who succeeded Innocent III resorted to the evolution of crusading ideology by including schismatics in the category of enemies of the Church. This context facilitated the supply of military forces to the Latin powers in Constantinople. Against the hostile Orthodox forces (Vlachs, Cumans, Bulgarians, Greeks etc.), the papacy called for the support of regional powers such as Hungary. Another measure adopted by the papacy and the Hungarian Kingdom consisted in the establishment of some permanent detachments of "crusaders" on the territory of Romania: Teutonic Knights in 1211 and Knights Hospitaller in 1247. The alliance of Latins and Hungarian kings against the Vlacho-Bulgarian state led by Asanids was based on the idea of a "substitute empire" that imitated Byzantium on a smaller scale. This idea was created by the members of a Romanian (Vlach) noble family known as Asen, whose intention was to revive the former Bulgarian state, the only legitimate political framework that could replace Byzantine rule. From the correspondence between Kaloyan and Innocent III it appears that the pope tried to diminish by diplomatic means the conflict between the Asanids, the Latin Empire of Constantinople and his ally, Hungary.[71]

The lack of a crusade terminology and privileges similar to those guaranteed to the Crusaders in the Holy Land suggests that there were some discrepancies between Rome and Riga regarding how the two sides perceived the conversion of Livonia. These discrepancies were partially eliminated by Honorius III, who fully supported the crusading idea in Livonia. More than his predecessor, Innocent III, Honorius allowed forced conversion by Albert and his knights. Besides offering a papal blessing, Honorius guaranteed the participants in the crusades that followed a plenary, not merely a partial, indulgence. Thus the crusaders in Livonia could enjoy the same privileges as those who fought in the Fifth Crusade. Even so, the crusade terminology shows that Honorius, like his predecessor, recommends the Crusaders in the Baltic region to use force only for the purpose of defending missionaries and the new converts. In 1240, Pope Gregory IX (1227–1241) continued Honorius' policy. However, he made several changes of an organizational nature. The first was to allow a full, unconditional commutation of vows from the Holy Land to the Baltic region. A second change was to support recruitment of new armed pilgrims by granting them indulgences. This was done through the sermons of the Dominican monks. A third change was to allow the Teutonic Order, who absorbed the Sword Brothers, to receive the income from redeemed vows. Furthermore, Gregory extended the geographical area from which the Dominicans could recruit knights for the Order's crusades.[72]

The ideological association between mission and crusade laid the foundations of a dualism between the bishopric led by Albert (also called Prince-Bishop of Livonia) and its clergy and the Sword Brothers. During the first two decades of the thirteenth century, the two allies managed to conquer all of Livonia and the southern part of Estonia. The new conquests led to disagreements concerning the division of territory. To these issues was added the dissatisfaction of the inhabitants of Riga. Both Albert and the Sword Brothers requested audiences with Innocent, who had to resolve the dispute. In the absence of a secular power capable of administering the new territories, Innocent decided that the Order would receive one-third of the conquered territory (Livonia and the Principality of Jersika, known as Lettia) and established the relationship between the Order and the Diocese of Riga. Thus the Sword Brothers did not have the right to perform any offensive military services in the new territories. The only situation in which the knights could intervene militarily was the defence of the Church and its members. Also, Volkwin, the Master of the Order, had to be vassal to the Bishop of Riga, whose authority was geographically limited to Livonia and Lettia. These territories were conquered "with the help of God" and could therefore only be administered by obedience to the pope.[73] However, all the possessions and rights of the Sword Brothers were confirmed by the German Emperor Frederick II (1220–1250) in May 1226.[74]

Innocent's interest in the conversion of Livonia is also confirmed by the visit of some papal legates such as Bishop William of Modena in 1226–1227. William was aware of the events in Livonia. He knew that the conversion process had suffered from pagan hostility. This also affected the Church's functioning. William was dissatisfied with the ecclesiastical organization in Livonia and therefore sought to impose order in the young and fragile Church.[75] One of his missions was to negotiate the distribution of authority between the Bishop of Riga and the Sword Brothers. However, Albert's death in 1229 led to a political destabilization in Livonia, which required a military reorganization, of great interest to Pope Gregory IX.[76]

The question of the truthfulness of the information provided by the chronicler Henry of Livonia has often been raised. In the thirteenth century, the inclusion of transcripts of papal or royal correspondence in various chronicles was a common practice. In Henry's citations, we have no evidence for the inclusion of any transcript of papal correspondence in his chronicle. The summary letters are rather superficial. Yet Henry was aware of the content of these letters, which could be discussed by clergy in Livonia. However, similarities between the contents of papal correspondence and Henry's mentions of papal privileges and crusades are extremely rare. The most relevant example is the description of a battle against the Livonians which took place in 1208 near Riga. The battle was part of a crusade, whose participants, according to Henry, received "plenary remissions of their neglected sins". Moreover, to encourage them, Bishop Albert promised them a "greater indulgence" and "eternal life".[77] What we may observe is that Innocent's correspondence makes no clear mention of a plenary indulgence, as Henry suggests. It is possible that the plenary indulgence mentioned by the chronicler is the one offered by his predecessor, Celestine III.

Notes

1 Contamine 2001: 103–104.
2 Jensen, Kurt V. 2001: 168.
3 For more details about the evolution of the Danish Church at the end of the twelfth century and the early thirteenth century, see Perron 2003: 182–212.
4 For more details about the Bernardine ecclesiastical network across Europe, see McGuire 1991: 75–132.
5 Burton and Kerr 2011: 48.
6 Christensen et al. 1976–1977, 1:3 no 34, pp. 47–49.
7 Christensen et al. 1976–1977, 1:3 no 81, 88, pp. 123–124, 130–131.
8 The Cistercian narratives are among the most important sources for Eskil's political and ecclesiastical profile. For his ecclesiastical career and his resignation, see Münster-Swendsen 2018: 51–68.
9 Saxo Grammaticus 2015: 14.55.3.
10 Christensen et al. 1976–1977, 1:3 no 26, p. 36.
11 Güttner-Sporzyński 2011: 256.

Expanding the crusading ideal 57

12 Johansen 1951: 90–94.
13 Christensen et al. 1976–1977, 1:3 no 28, pp. 38–39.
14 Christensen et al. 1976–1977, 1:3 no 91, pp. 139–141.
15 Jaakkola 1951: 83–111.
16 *Non parum animus noster affligitur et amaritudine non modica et dolore torquetur, cum feritatem Estonum et aliorum paganorum illarum partium adversus dei fideles et Christianae fidei cultores, gravius insurgere et immanius debacchari audimus, et christiani nominis impugnare virtutem.* Christensen et al. 1976–1977, 1:3 no 27, pp. 37–38.
17 Christensen et al. 1976–1977, 1:3 no 29, pp. 40–41.
18 Christensen et al. 1976–1977, 1:3 no 81, pp. 123–124.
19 Iben Fonnesberg 2007: 76–77.
20 *Quorum promissis Kanutus securius quam cautius aestimatis, concilio ocius dimisso, in Iutiam secessit, fortissimis quibusque Scanorum ac Sialandensium tantam otii tranquillitatem causantibus seque nimia iam quiete in desidiam provolvi querentibus; longo deliciarum usu enerves animos gerere, qui sub rege Waldemaro totius ferme anni tempus multiplici rerum agitatione varioque militiae genere deducere consueverint. Nam militaris roboris nervos, sicut otio hebetari ac remitti, ita negotio intendi excitarique. Igitur acuendae virtutis gratia piraticam adversum Estones in commune decerni placuit.* Saxo Grammaticus 2015: 16.4.3.
21 *Verum quamquam Sueones ac Dani inimicitias gererent, ne destinatam paganis cladem Christianis infligerent, insulae parcendum duxerunt, religionis concordiam regnorum odiis praeferentes. Hic ab indigenis permixtos Estonibus Curos propinquo in portu piraticam exercere perdocti, indicatum sibi locum, ut cuique navigationis celeritas suppetebat, cum contemptu hostium, regii monitus immemores, certatim subintrant. Quo viso, speculatrix Estonum ratis remigio in altum excessit deviaque navigatione diffugere quam sociae classi visorum nuntium afferre maluit.* Saxo Grammaticus 2015: 14.40.3.
22 Bugiani 2016: lines 357–366, pp. 60–61.
23 For a useful summary of the *Chronicle*'s basic attributes in a discussion on the manuscript tradition, structure and intended audience, see Murray 2001: 235–251.
24 Henry of Livonia 1874: 2.10.13.
25 Bugiani 2016: lines 2422–2429, pp. 164–165.
26 Saxo Grammaticus 2015: 15.4.1; 16.1.2.
27 Sawyer 1993: 115, Berend 2007: 199–200.
28 Berend 2007: 200.
29 Line 2007: 94, Bysted et al. 2012: 143.
30 Sephton 1899: 22.113.
31 Andrea 2000: 9–19.
32 Cipollone 2003: PL 215, 1500–1503, pp. 524–527.
33 Riley-Smith 1987: 141.
34 Teulié and Lux-Sterritt 2009: 6. The name comes from the Latin word *mendicare* "to beg" and refers to the fact that members of the mendicant orders could ensure their existence through the help of their audience who

provided them with food and those things necessary for life. Unlike the Benedictines and Cistercians, mendicant orders embraced an ascetic, poor, often itinerant lifestyle. A first condition was the renunciation of all wealth and the spread of the message of Christ through preaching in the cities. Their maxim was *non sibi soli vivere sed et aliis proficere* ("not to live only for oneself but to benefit others as well"). The main mendicant orders are the Franciscans and the Dominicans. For more details about the history of these two orders, and the relationship between written and visual sources, see the collection of studies edited by Cornelison, Debby and Howard 2016. For the mendicant orders and their involvement in the crusades, see Hamilton 1995: 693–712.

35 Henderson 1896: 337–344.
36 For further details, see Selart 2015.
37 Henry of Livonia 1874: 1.1–3.
38 For more details regarding Meinhard's ecclesiastical activity, see Munzinger 2006: 163–185.
39 Henry of Livonia 1874: 1.10.
40 *Summus itaque pontifex audito numero baptizatorum non eos deserendos censuit, sed ad observationem fidei, quam sponte promiserant, cogendos decrevit. Remissionem quippe omnium peccatorum indulsit omnibus, qui ad resuscitandam illam primitivam ecclesiam accepta cruce transeant.* Henry of Livonia 1874: 1.12.
41 For the sacralization of Livonia as the domain of the Mother of God, see Tamm 2013: 431–455.
42 *Lyvoniensis ecclesie ruinam tam domno pape quam metropolitano et Christi fidelibus conqueritur universis. Igitur domnus papa cunctis signum crucis accipientibus et contra perfidos Lyvones se armantibus remissionem indulget peccatorum, litteras super hiis eidem episcopo Bertoldo sicut et suo dirigens predecessori.* Henry of Livonia 1874: 2.3.
43 Henry of Livonia 1874: 2.4–7.
44 *Quem tamen conventum regularium et episcopalem sedem postea Albertus episcopus de Ykescola in Rigam tercio sue consecrationis anno transtulit et cathedram episcopalem cum tota Lyvonia beatissime Dei genitricis Marie honori deputavit.* Henry of Livonia 1874: 3.6.4. The city's cathedral was built in 1221.
45 Henry of Livonia stated that Theodoric was the founder of the Order. Other sources claim that the founder is Bishop Albert. However, after the Lithuanians defeated the Sword Brothers at Saule in 1237, the members who survived joined the larger Teutonic Order. Rogers 2010: 83. A major contribution to the Order's history is the work of Benninghoven 1965.
46 *Eodem tempore previdens idem frater Theodericus perfidiam Lyvonum et multitudini paganorum non posse resistere metuens, et ideo ad multiplicandum numerum fidelium et ad conservandam in gentibus ecclesiam fratres quosdam milicie Christi instituit, quibus domnus papa Innocencius regulam Templariorum commisit et signum in veste ferendum dedit, scilicet gladium et crucem, et sub obedientia sui episcopi esse mandavit.* Henry of Livonia 1874: 3.6.6.

47 Maier 1998: 45.
48 *Post consecrationem estate proxima Gothlandiam vadit et ibidem circa quingentos viros signo crucis ad eundum in Lyvoniam signat. Inde per Daciam transiens munera regis Canuti et ducis Woldemari et Absolonis archiepiscopi recepit.* Henry of Livonia 1874: 3.2–3.
49 *Et coram eodem rege in sentencia queritur, si bona in Lyvoniam peregrinancium sub tuicione pape ponantur, sicut eorum, qui Ierosolimam vadunt. Responsum vero est ea sub protectione apostolici comprehendi, qui peregrinacionem Lyvonie in plenariam peccaminum iniungens vie coequavit Ierosolimitane.* Henry of Livonia 1874: 3.2.
50 Fletcher 1999: 493–494.
51 In the early thirteenth century, the population of Riga was about 6,000–7,000 inhabitants. Selart 2019: 43–44, 47, 56.
52 Jensen, Carsten S. 2017: 77.
53 Fletcher 1999: 495.
54 Bombi 2005: 232–237.
55 *Cauponem nomine, qui quasi rex et senior Lyvonum de Thoreyda, secum assumit et magna parte Theuthonie perlustrata tandem eum Romam duxit et apostolico exhibet. Quem apostolicus benignissime recipiens deosculatur et de statu gencium circa Lyvoniam existencium multa perquirens pro conversione gentis Lyvonice Deo plurimum congratulatur.* Henry of Livonia 1874: 3.7.5–6.
56 After 1300, Riga ceased to be a popular destination for German pilgrims. Selart 2019: 49.
57 The event could be placed in the context of the conflict between Welfs and Staufen. Nielsen 2001: 113–115.
58 Christensen et al. 1976–1977, 1:3 no 254, pp. 400–401.
59 Henry of Livonia 1874: 3.10.10.
60 Henry of Livonia 1874: 3.21.4.
61 Fonnesberg-Schmidt 2011: 220.
62 For further details regarding Innocent's preaching for the Livonian mission, see Bombi 2005: 232–241.
63 "Therefore go and make disciples of all nations, baptizing them in the name of the Father and of the Son and of the Holy Spirit, and teaching them to obey everything I have commanded you". Matthew 28:19–20.
64 For the parable (also called the "Parable of the Labourers in the Vineyard" or the "Parable of the Generous Employer"), see Matthew 20:1–16. The pope uses quotation from John's gospel to suggest the divine reward received by missionaries. "Don't you have a saying, 'It's still four months until harvest'? I tell you, open your eyes and look at the fields! They are ripe for harvest. Even now the one who reaps draws a wage and harvests a crop for eternal life, so that the sower and the reaper may be glad together. Thus the saying 'One sows and another reaps' is true. I sent you to reap what you have not worked for. Others have done the hard work, and you have reaped the benefits of their labour." John 4:35–38.

60 Expanding the crusading ideal

65 *Transactis diebus aliquantis idem venerabilis papa Innocencius predicto Cauponi dona sua, videlicet centum aureos, porrigit et in Theuttoniam redire volenti magno caritatis affectu valedicens benedicit et bibliotecam beati Gregorii pape manu scriptam episcopo Lyvoniensi pei fratrem Theodericum mittit.* Henry of Livonia 1874: 3.7.6.
66 For further details about the Gregorian mission to Britain, see Wood 1994: 1–17.
67 For more details regarding the conversion model followed by Innocent III, see Egger 2004: 13–46, Doran 2003: 56–73.
68 Dragnea 2015: 46.
69 The *Regula pastoralis* had for the secular clergy the same importance that the *Regula Benedicti* had for monks. Marie-Louise Laudage believes that from the time of Gregory I until the final phase of the Investiture controversy, there were two main aspects that defined a bishop: *caritas* ("charity", with social and spiritual implications) and *memoria* ("memory"), seen as one of the most important episcopal obligations. For more details, see Laudage 1993: 262–288, 307–317.
70 Innocent's letter issued on 21 January 1205 was translated and commented by Moore 2003: 138.
71 For further details on the relationship between the papacy and the Vlacho-Bulgarian state, see Papacostea 1993: 11–48. For the imperial idea adopted by the Asanids, the rulers of a successor state of the Byzantine Empire, see Madgearu 2016: 95.
72 Fonnesberg-Schmidt 2007: 247.
73 Sommerlechner 2015: no. 139 (141), pp. 224–226.
74 Strehlke 1869: no. 235, p. 229.
75 Fletcher 1999: 495.
76 Maier 1998: 45–46.
77 *Episcopus interim in Dunemunde a vento contrario detentus, cognita suorum interfectione et ecclesie sue intellecta traditione, peregrinos omnes in unum convocat, ecclesie dampna lacrimando indicat et, ut fiant ecclesie defensores et fortes auxiliarii, ipsos invitat et crucis signum resumere in plenariam ante neglectorum delictorum remissionem ammonendo confortat et ob maioris laboris sui longam peregrinationem maiorem indulgenciam et vitam promittit eternam.* Henry of Livonia 1874: 3.11. 9.

References

Andrea, Alfred J. 2000. *Contemporary Sources for the Fourth Crusade.* Leiden: Brill.
Benninghoven, Friedrich. 1965. *Der Orden der Schwertbrüder: Fratres Milicie Christi de Livonia.* Cologne: Böhlau.
Berend, Nora. 2007. *Christianization and the Rise of Christian Monarchy: Scandinavia, Central Europe and Rus' c.900–1200.* Cambridge: Cambridge University Press.

Expanding the crusading ideal 61

Bombi, Barbara. 2005. 'Innocent III and the *praedicatio* to the Heathens in Livonia (1198–1204)'. In *Medieval History Writing and Crusading Ideology*, eds. Tuomas M. S. Lehtonen and Kurt V. Jensen, 232–237. Helsinki: Finnish Literature Society.

Bugiani, Piero (ed. and trans.). 2016. *Cronaca rimata della Livonia: Livländische Reimchronik (XIII sec.)*. Viterbo: Vocifuoriscena.

Burton, Janet E. and Kerr, Julie. 2011. *The Cistercians in the Middle Ages*. Woodbridge: Boydell Press.

Bysted, Ane et al. 2012. *Jerusalem in the North: Denmark and the Baltic Crusades, 1100–1522*. Turnhout: Brepols.

Christensen, C. A., Nielsen, Herluf and Weibull, Lauritz (eds.). 1976–1977. *Diplomatarium Danicum*. Copenhagen: C.A. Reitzel.

Cipollone, Giulio. 2003. *Cristianità-Islam: cattività e liberazione in nome di Dio. Il tempo di Innocenzo III dopo "il 1187"*, Seconda ristampa. Rome: Pontificia Univ. Gregoriana.

Contamine, Philippe. 2001. 'Un război contra împărăției cerurilor'. In *Cruciadele*, ed. Michel Balard, 99–108. Bucharest: Artemis.

Cornelison, S. J., Debby, N. Ben-Aryeh and Howard, P. F. 2016. *Mendicant Cultures in the Medieval and Early Modern World: Word, Deed, and Image*. Turnhout: Brepols.

Doran, John. 2003. 'In Whose Footsteps? The Role Models of Innocent III'. In *Innocenzo III: Urbs et Orbis*, 55, ed. A. Sommerlechner, 56–73. Rome: Società romana di storia patria.

Dragnea, Mihai. 2015. 'Otto din Bamberg: Reformă Monastică și Misiune Apostolică'. In *Timp, societate și identitate culturală: „Miniaturi" istorice*, eds. Ileana Căzan and Bogdan Mateescu, 25–48. Cluj-Napoca: Academia Română – Centrul de Studii Transilvane.

Egger, Christoph. 2004. 'The Growling of the Lion and the Humming of the Fly: Gregory the Great and Innocent III'. In *Pope, Church and City: Essays in Honour of Brenda M. Bolton*, eds. Frances Andrews, Christoph Egger and Constance Rousseau, 13–46. Leiden: Brill.

Ernest F. Henderson (trans. and ed.). 1896. *Select Historical Documents of the Middle Ages*. New York: G. Bell.

Fletcher, Richard A. 1999. *The Barbarian Conversion: From Paganism to Christianity*. Berkeley and Los Angeles: University of California Press.

Fonnesberg-Schmidt, Iben. 2007. *The Popes and the Baltic Crusades: 1147–1254*. Leiden-Boston: Brill.

Fonnesberg-Schmidt, Iben. 2011. 'Riga and Rome: Henry of Livonia and the Papal Curia'. In *Crusading and Chronicle Writing on the Medieval Baltic Frontier: A Companion to the Chronicle of Henry of Livonia*, eds. Marek Tamm, Linda Kaljundi and Carsten Selch Jensen, 209–228. Aldershot: Ashgate.

Güttner-Sporzyński, Darius von. 2011. 'Poland and the Papacy Before the Second Crusade'. In *La Papauté et les croisades/The Papacy and the Crusades: actes du VIIe congrès de la Society for the Study of the Crusades and the Latin*

East/Proceedings of the VIIth Conference of the Society for the Crusades and the Latin East, ed. Michel Balard, 255–268. Farnham: Ashgate.
Hamilton, Bernard. 1995. 'Ideals of Holiness: Crusaders, Contemplatives, and Mendicants'. *The International History Review* 17/4: 693–712.
Henry of Livonia. 1874. *Heinrici Chronicon Lyvoniae*, ed. Georg Heinrich Pertz, *MGH*. Hanover: Impensis Bibliopolii Hahniani.
Jaakkola, Jalmari. 1951. 'Suomen ensimmäinen piispa'. *Turun Historiallinen Arkisto* 11: 83–111.
Jensen, Carsten S. 2017. 'Urban Life and the Crusades in North Germany and the Baltic Lands in the Early Thirteenth Century'. In *Crusade and Conversion on the Baltic Frontier 1150–1500*, ed. Alan V. Murray, 75–94. London: Routledge.
Jensen, Kurt V. 2001. 'Denmark and the Second Crusade: The Formation of a Crusader State'. In *The Second Crusade: Scope and Consequences*, eds. Jonathan Phillips and Martin Hoch, 164–179. Manchester: Manchester University Press.
Johansen, Paul. 1951. *Nordische Mission: Revals Gründung und die Schwedensiedlung in Estland*. Stockholm: Wahlström & Widstrand.
Laudage, Marie-Louise. 1993. *Caritas und Memoria mittelalterlicher Bischöfe*, Münstersche Historische Forschungen 3. Cologne: Böhlau.
Line, Philip. 2007. *Kingship and State Formation in Sweden: 1130–1290*. Leiden: Brill.
Madgearu, Alexandru. 2016. *The Asanids: The Political and Military History of the Second Bulgarian Empire (1185–1280)*. Leiden: Brill.
Maier, Christoph T. 1998. *Preaching the Crusades: Mendicant Friars and the Cross in the Thirteenth Century*. Cambridge: Cambridge University Press.
McGuire, Brian P. 1991. *The Difficult Saint: Bernard of Clairvaux and his Tradition*. Kalamazoo: Cistercian Publications.
Moore, John C. 2003. *Pope Innocent III (1160/61–1216): To Root Up and to Plant*. Leiden: Brill.
Munzinger, Mark R. 2006. 'The Profits of the Cross: Merchant Involvement in the Baltic Crusade (c. 1180–1230)'. *Journal of Medieval History* 32: 163–185.
Murray, Alan V. 2001. 'The Structure, Genre and Intended Audience of *The Livonian Rhymed Chronicle*'. In *Crusade and Conversion on the Baltic Frontier, 1150–1500*, ed. Alan V. Murray, 235–251. Alderhsot: Routledge.
Münster-Swendsen, Mia. 2018. 'History, Politics and Canon Law: The Resignation of Archbishop Eskil of Lund'. In *The Use of Canon Law in Ecclesiastical Administration, 1000–1234*, eds. Melodie H. Eichbauer and Danica Summerlin, 51–68. Leiden: Brill.
Nielsen, Torben K. 2001. 'The Missionary Man: Archbishop Anders Sunesen and the Baltic Crusade, 1206–21'. In *Crusade and Conversion on the Baltic Frontier, 1150–1500*, ed. Alan V. Murray, 95–117. Alderhsot: Ashgate.
Papacostea, Șerban. 1993. *Românii în secolul al XIII-lea. Între cruciată și Imperiul Mongol*. Bucharest: Enciclopedică.

Perron, Anthony. 2003. 'Metropolitan Might and Papal Power on the Latin-Christian Frontier: Transforming the Danish Church around the Time of the Fourth Lateran Council'. *The Catholic Historical Review* 89/2: 182–212.
Riley-Smith, Jonathan. 1987. *The Crusades: A Short History*. New Haven and London: Yale University Press.
Rogers, Clifford J. (ed.). 2010. *The Oxford Encyclopedia of Medieval Warfare and Military Technology*, Vol. 1. Oxford: Oxford University Press.
Sawyer, Birgit. 1993. *Medieval Scandinavia: From Conversion to Reformation, Circa 800–1500*. Minneapolis and London: University of Minnesota Press.
Saxo Grammaticus. 2015. *Gesta Danorum: The History of the Danes*, ed. Karsten Friis Jensen, trans. Peter Fisher, 2 vols. Oxford: Oxford University Press.
Selart, Anti. 2015. *Livonia, Rus' and the Baltic Crusades in the Thirteenth Century*. Leiden: Brill.
Selart, Anti. 2019. 'Where Was the Home of the Livonian Merchant? Early Urban Mobility in the Baltics'. *Zapiski Historyczne* 84/1: 43–66.
Sephton, J. (trans.). 1899. *Sverrissaga: The Saga of King Sverri of Norway*. London: David Nutt.
Sommerlechner, Andrea et al. 2015. *Die Register Innocenz' III., 13. Pontifikatsjahr, 1210/1211: Texte und Indices*, 139 (141). Vienna: Österreichische Akademie.
Strehlke, Ernst. 1869. *Tabulae ordinis Theutonici ex tabularii regii Berolinensis codice potissimum*. Berlin: Weidmann.
Tamm, Marek. 2013. 'How to Justify a Crusade? The Conquest of Livonia and New Crusade Rhetoric in the Early Thirteenth Century'. *Journal of Medieval History* 39: 431–455.
Teulié, Gilles and Lux-Sterritt, Laurence. 2009. *War Sermons*. Newcastle: Cambridge Scholars.
Wood, Ian. 1994. 'The Mission of Augustine of Canterbury to the English'. *Speculum* 69/1: 1–17.

Conclusion

A distinct feature of the early crusades was the question of how to morally and legally justify a religious war against enemies of the Church such as apostates. During the twelfth century, the Church strongly accepted the use of force against apostates, in the same way that it accepted it against heretics or infidels. In the case of the Wends, they were seen as apostates because they rejected the Empire of the Saxon Christ. This meant they rejected *fides christiana*. Therefore the Saxon clergy and apologists like Bernard understood that the Wendish uprisings led not only to a religious apostasy, but also to a political one. We do not know how much the Saxon nobles understood the religious dimension of the campaign across the Elbe or how much were they interested in the conversion. What we know is that Bernard gave assurances that conversion would not be an effect of the military conquest, but a spiritual endeavor of the ecclesiastical authorities who led the crusade. In this way, a conquest followed a "rightful intention" (*intentio recta*), and the Saxons' actions were blessed by the pope. From Bernard's speech we can see that he acted both as a mediator in the conflict with the eastern neighbours, and as an element of connection between the juridical and moral dimension of the crusade.

In theory, a crusade was no ordinary pilgrimage nor a military campaign. The crusade against the Wends could be seen as a sort of experiment conducted by the papacy. However, the apologists had difficulties in justifying a war without religious benefits. The difficulties were based on the fact that across the Elbe were no sacred shrines to be protected. This was an easier task for the initiators and apologists of the Livonian Crusade.[1] Most of the crusaders who fought in Livonia came from Saxony. That means they must already have been familiar with the crusading model that was implemented against the Wends. When a war could be placed in a religious context, the clergy had less difficulty. The moral and legal justification came from theology. The crusading

Conclusion 65

ideology was a good basis, allowing any conflict involving religious interests to be considered a holy war. The crusade forced the Saxon nobles to renounce the tributary relations with their eastern neighbours. By joining Christendom, the Wends followed the model of vassalic relationships. This new status would prevent possible insurrections and be materially beneficial to both the nobility and the ecclesiastical authorities.

The crusade against the Wends was morally justified by divine vengeance. The zeal which came from God functioned as an emotional fuel for knights. Their actions did not violate canon law because they were driven by sincere emotions. What was moral for the clergy was also considered legal for the laity, so the punishment of the Wends for their atrocities against Christians became human justice. The legal justification was based on the formal status of the Wends. Their apostasy was not only religious, but also political. The arguments used by contemporary writers were not taken from treaties concluded between the Saxon nobles and Wendish princes. For the clergy, religious apostasy meant a violation of any written or verbal agreement. Since the medieval concept of the state followed a Christian model, the Bible was the main source of juridical inspiration. The moral justification was based on just emotions which were taken from the Old Testament. The most common was the crusader's zeal, which was manifest in love for God or as a desire for revenge. Even if these collective emotions had to be sincere, they would not have come by free will. If the emotions were not based on material interests but only on faith, then the crusader's actions were morally justified.

The military protection of the Saxon and Danish knights provided a basis for the expansion of both trading and missionary activities on the eastern shores of the Baltic. While a missionary tradition existed from Hamburg-Bremen and Magdeburg in the Wendish territory, in Livonia, Christian mission activities were often intertwined with political interests.

Note

1 Tamm, Marek. 2013. 'How to Justify a Crusade? The Conquest of Livonia and New Crusade Rhetoric in the Early Thirteenth Century'. *Journal of Medieval History* 39: 431–455.

Index of names

Absalon, bishop of Roskilde and archbishop of Lund 20, 39–41, 43, 45, 49
Adalbero, archbishop of Hamburg–Bremen 8, 21
Adam of Bremen, chronicler 2, 19, 33, 50
Adelgot, archbishop of Magdeburg 32, 34
Adolf II, count of Holstein 7, 10–13, 21–22
Adrian IV, Pope 40, 45
Albert the Bear, count of Ballenstedt and margrave of the North March 7, 10, 15–16
Albert, Livonian bishop 47–52, 54–56, 58
Aleksander, bishop of Płock 42
Alexander III, Pope 40–45
Amandus, bishop of Tongeren–Maastricht 50
Anders Sunesen, archbishop of Lund 45
Anselm, theologian and archbishop of Canterbury 31
Anselm, bishop of Havelberg, papal legate 14, 17
Anselm, bishop of Lucca 30
Asen (Asanids), Vlach dynasty of the Vlacho–Bulgarian state 54
Augustine of Hippo, theologian 23–24, 30–31, 53

Bernard of Clairvaux, Cistercian abbot 2, 5–10, 12–14, 21–22, 24–25, 35, 40, 64

Bernard I, bishop of Hildesheim 7
Bernard II, Saxon duke 33
Berthold of Hanover, Livonian bishop 47–48
Bolesław III, Polish king 23, 34–35, 42
Bolesław IV, Polish duke 34
Bruno of Querfurt, missionary bishop and martyr 21

Canute Lavard, Danish prince and the first duke of Schleswig 41
Canute V, Danish king 23
Canute VI, Danish king 44, 46, 49
Casimir I, Polish duke 34
Caupo, Livonian leader 50–52
Celestine III, Pope 44, 48, 56
Charlemagne, Frankish emperor 2, 25
Christian of Oliva, Cistercian monk 36
Clementia, Saxon duchess, wife of Henry the Lion 11, 13
Clement III, Pope 47
Conrad I, duke of Masovia 36
Conrad III, German king 1, 10, 36

Ebo, hagiographer 53
Eligius, bishop of Noyon 50
Emmehard, bishop of Mecklenburg 13
Enrico, cardinal of Ostia 39
Erik X, Swedish king 45
Eirik Sigurdson, Norwegian prince 46
Eskil, archbishop of Lund 12, 39–42, 45

Index of names

Eugene III, Pope 1–2, 5, 10, 13–15, 43–44, 48
Evermod, bishop of Ratzeburg 20
Eystein, archbishop of Nidaros (Trondheim) 42

Folquinus, semimythical bishop of Finland 43
Frederick I Barbarossa, German emperor 11, 14, 40
Frederick II, German emperor 39, 55
Fulco, bishop of Estonia 42–43

Gallus Anonymous, chronicler 35
Gelasius I, Pope 16
Gerhard, archbishop of Hamburg–Bremen 51
Gerold, bishop of Oldenburg 10
Gneuomir, Pomeranian prince 23
Gottschalk, Obotrite prince 3, 33, 50
Gratian, theologian 23, 31
Gregory I, Pope 23, 52–53, 60
Gregory IX, Pope 55–56

Hartwig I, archbishop of Hamburg–Bremen 8, 13
Hartwig II, archbishop of Hamburg–Bremen 47–48
Helmold of Bosau, chronicler and priest 2, 5, 7–8, 11–14, 19, 21–22, 31–32, 50
Henry I, German king 2
Henry II, German king and emperor 21
Henry V, German king and emperor 34
Henry of Badewide, count of Ratzeburg 20–21
Henry the Lion, Saxon duke 7–8, 10–14, 20–22
Henry of Livonia, chronicler 44, 47–50, 52, 56
Herbord, hagiographer 53
Honorius III, Pope 51, 54–55
Hugh of Payens, Grand Master of the Templars 6
Huguccio, theologian 24, 39

Innocent III, Pope 36, 45–46, 49–56

Jakub of Żnin, archbishop of Gniezno 42
John, bishop of Mecklenburg 33

Karl Sverkersson, Swedish king 45
Kaloyan, Vlach tsar of the Vlacho–Bulgarian state 54

Leo IX, Pope 30
Lothair of Supplinburg, German duke, king and emperor 34, 41
Louis the Pious, Frankish emperor 20

Meinhard, first bishop of Livonia 46–48, 51
Michał Adwaniec, chancellor 42

Nako, Obotrite dynasty 3
Nicolaus, monk 42–43
Niklot, Obotrite prince 7, 10–13, 22

Otto I, German emperor 3
Otto III, German emperor 3
Otto, bishop of Bamberg 23, 42, 53
Ozur Perst, cleric 46

Peter of Celle, abbot of St. Remi at Reims 40, 42–43
Philip of Swabia, German king 49
Pribislav, Obotrite prince of Wagria 10, 50
Pribislav, Obotrite prince of Mecklenburg, son of Niklot 13

Riedegost, Wendish god 33
Robert the Monk, chronicler and cleric 25, 33
Robert II, count of Flanders 32
Rotholph, priest and monk 22
Rudolf II, count of Stade 8
Rufinus of Bologna, theologian 24

Saladin, sultan of Egypt and Syria 35
Saxo Grammaticus, chronicler 11, 20, 22, 41, 44–45
Sigebert of Gembloux, chronicler 7, 25
Stefan, Cistercian monk from the abbey of Alvastra 45
Sverker II, Swedish king 45

Index of names

Sverre, Norwegian king 46
Sweyn III, Danish king 11, 20, 23

Theodoric, Cistercian monk from the abbey of Loccum 47, 49–50, 52, 58
Thomas Becket, archbishop of Canterbury 40–41

Urban II, Pope 5, 25

Valdemar I, Danish king 11, 20, 23, 40–41, 44
Valdemar II, Danish king 44, 49, 51
Wibald, abbot of Stavelot and Corvey 7, 14
Vicelin, bishop of Oldenburg 3, 13, 47
Victor IV, antipope 40

Vincent, chronicler and bishop of Cracow 23, 34–35
Vincent of Prague, chronicler, notary and canon of Prague cathedral 8
Vitus (St.), the patron of the Corvey monastery 20
Vladimir Vseslavich, prince of Polotsk 47
Volkwin, master of the Livonian Brothers 55
Vratislav, son of Niklot 13

William, bishop of Modena and papal legate 55
Wojciech (Adalbert), the chaplain of Bolesław III and bishop of Cammin 42

For Product Safety Concerns and Information please contact our EU representative GPSR@taylorandfrancis.com
Taylor & Francis Verlag GmbH, Kaufingerstraße 24, 80331 München, Germany

www.ingramcontent.com/pod-product-compliance
Lightning Source LLC
Chambersburg PA
CBHW070741230426
43669CB00014B/2540